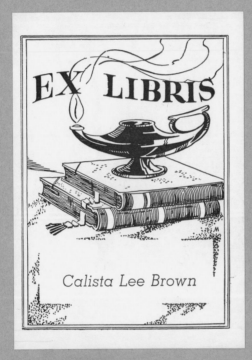

EX LIBRIS

Calista Lee Brown

Every Girl Is Entitled to a Husband

Books by Nina Farewell

———————◆———————

EVERY GIRL IS ENTITLED TO A HUSBAND

THE UNFAIR SEX

SOMEONE TO LOVE

Every Girl
Is Entitled

by NINA FAREWELL

New York   Toronto   London

to a Husband

drawings by Roy Doty

McGraw-Hill Book Company, Inc.

To Mr. J. C. Reynolds darling

Contents

1. Is Love Necessary?   1

2. Why Don't the Men Propose, Mama?
   Why Don't the Men Propose?   6

3. Preparation for the Hunt   11
   Sedatives for the conscience
   Tonics for the spirit
   The 15 pleasures of wifehood

4. Sex   22
   The great male humbuggery

The bad effects of false padding
Plumbing the male libido
A rudimentary exercise in spying
How to muddle through in the dark
Sexual compatibility
Putting sex in its proper place

5. Where to Look for Him   38
Geographic location
Careers
Friendship
Vacation and travel
The matchmaker
The amateur matchmaker
Adult education
Education
Pastimes

6. The Dikdook   66

7. Camouflage   76
The tall girl
The old girl
The plain girl

8. How to Trap Him   84

9. The Lures   87
Home and hearth
Fair damsel to the rescue
Miss Patience
Sick sick sick
Big name hunter

Green apples
Fountain of youth

10. The Traps   102
    The confidence game
    The great deception
    Come into my parlor
    No no no
    Shadow play
    The helpmeet
    Stolen sweets
    The mouse trap

11. The Formula   118
    Generalissima
    The woodpecker
    Cool, cool shoulder
    Little girl lost
    Fifiola
    Minerva
    You're mine!
    Peter and Wendy
    The opportunist

12. Love Potions   133
    Variation A: Fire and Tears
    Variation B: Bittersweet
    Variation C: Milk and honey
    Variation D: Manna

13. Spellbinders   141
    Gold

Glamour
Prestige
Aphrodite
The enchanted circle

14. How to Design Your Own Method   151

15. For the Career-minded Girl   154

16. Girls! Fasten Your Chastity Belts   165

17. What to Do if You Didn't   171
Tragedietta
Caprice
Mea culpa
Gloriana
Good deportment for naughty girls

18. Pitfalls and How to Avoid Them   182

19. Kindness in Victory   195

Every Girl Is Entitled to a Husband

. . . 'Tis your glorious duty to seek it!

To seek it with thimbles, to seek it with care:
To pursue it with forks and hope;
To threaten its life with a railway-share;
To charm it with smiles and soap!

LEWIS CARROLL

ONE

——————◆•◆——————

Is Love Necessary?

THOSE WHO speak the Truth have always invited criticism. For daring to set forth on these pages Facts rarely mentioned in polite society, and for attacking the Fancies cherished by all nice people, I shall probably be labeled vulgar, insensitive, and unwomanly. This is to be expected when one insists on being realistic in a romantic world.

And what a romantic world it is! Surely the twentieth century will go down in history as the Era of Eros. By comparison, the Age of Chivalry seems almost prosaic. Love in that time was a tidbit, a delicacy reserved for the high-born few; today it is the bread of the masses. We are enchanted with it. We are obsessed by it. We demand it in the theater

1

and the cinema, in books, magazines and newspapers, and in the lives of public figures. Even the most commonplace commodities can be sold only by appealing to the popular taste for Love, Love, and more Love.

To such lengths do we carry our love-madness that we insist on dragging it into the area of matrimony. In other centuries marriages were contracted for the sake of propriety, propagation, and property rights. Today we disdain those who marry for old-fashioned reasons, and esteem only the man or woman who makes a romantic match.

The modern girl, growing up in this love-sodden atmos-

2

phere, is convinced she must love and be loved if she would marry with honor—a destructive credo which leads to many cases of spinsterhood. Is a woman to remain unwed because she is not capable of falling in love? Or because she cannot inspire a man to fall in love with her? Or because she cannot find her ideal? No, no, no!

 ## Every girl is entitled to a husband

It is her eternal right to have a legal hold on a man, to wear a wedding ring, and to bear the title of Mrs. And if this cannot be accomplished *with* love, then it must be accomplished *without*.

Do not make the mistake of thinking I am an enemy of love. I have been beguiled by it, tormented and enslaved by it all my life, and I say any girl who can make a

MARRIAGE WITH LOVE

should do so and God bless her. That girl has found the Bluebird of Happiness. I wish only to point out that a union is both possible and respectable *without* benefit of the grand passion.

This may be a shocking idea on first consideration. The very phrase,

MARRIAGE WITHOUT LOVE

has a disreputable look. Nevertheless, I am going to ask that every unmarried female read the following aloud: "I can marry without love." Do you find such a sentence difficult to voice? Force yourself. Now, say it over and over again. Observe how the shock value gradually diminishes. After a while the words will drop from your lips as easily as How-do-you-do. What is more, you will come to believe in them. And having rid yourself of the *idée fixe* of your generation, you will find the path to the altar considerably eased.

However, these are radical thoughts and should be hidden away in your most secret heart. In view of the romantic temper of the times, it is unpolitic to admit to so practical an attitude toward marriage. The girl who is discreet will not reveal herself to anyone—not to her friends, not to her parents, and above all not to a prospective mate. Whatever her reason for marrying, she will swear that it is Love.

Do not cry "Fie!" Willingness to practice deception is a symptom of the mature mind. It is "mature" to crave the approval of Society and to do whatever is necessary to earn that approval. In a period when it is fashionable to exhibit curves the girl who goes forth flat is showing contempt for her fellowman. When it is *comme il faut* to be flat-chested, every decent female binds herself tight, and only a vulgar one is buxom.

Life is filled with examples of this type of civilized appeasement. For instance, although the male was fashioned by nature to ". . . roam over the earth impregnating as many females as he possibly can" * he is forbidden to do so. He is obliged instead to marry one woman and remain faithful to her always. This rigid channeling of his powers is of course bitterly resented. Yet, the man who is mature does not fight against the arbitrary curtailment of his activities,

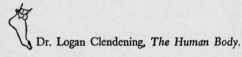 Dr. Logan Clendening, *The Human Body.*

4

nor does he flaunt his defiance. No. He pays lip service to Convention and quietly renders unto Nature what is hers.

In this manner must each one make the necessary adjustment between what is and what ought to be. And the girl who feigns love for the man she marries is not a hypocrite but an integrated member of Society. Moreover, if she pretends with deep sincerity she may find she has convinced herself as well as everyone else. How often I have heard my Grandmother say, "A girl who has any sense at all, manages to be in love with the man who asks her!"

TWO

Why Don't the Men Propose, Mama? Why Don't the Men Propose? *

ACTUALLY, if put to the test, few girls are so stubborn they would remain spinsters rather than pretend to love the man who asks them. The problem is—

IT IS NOT SO EASY TO BE ASKED!

According to popular fancy, every maiden has two or more suitors and when she is ready to wed, she need only decide which one she really and truly loves. Some fortunate females do find themselves in this position, but they are the exception. The vast majority are faced with the task of

 From the poem by Thomas Payne Bayly (1797–1839).

1. Locating a man.
2. Attracting him.
3. Luring him into matrimony.

At first glance it appears that this program goes against the Law of Nature. For in the animal kingdom it is the male, not the female, who is the pursuer. But we are speaking here of the Law of Society, not the Law of Nature, which is immutable. On the animal level man behaves exactly as his animal brethren—he prowls and preens, proffers gifts, battles competitors, and in countless ways exerts himself to win the female. However, on the animal level, pursuit of the female is for the purpose of *possession*, not *marriage*. When we speak of marriage we move into a different realm. The fact is that

MARRIAGE IS A STRICTLY
HUMAN INVENTION

There is no parallel to it among the beasts. No creature, wild or domestic, is bound to its mate by a contract which gives valuable privileges to the female and imposes onerous duties on the male. How can we speak of the Law of Nature when speaking of Marriage? The two are incompatible.

Let us be grateful for the animal urge that compels the human male to pursue the female. It brings him into close range, and while he is busy conniving to satisfy his primitive needs she can capture him to satisfy her civilized ones.

If the human female must lure the male into matrimony, let her do so proudly, without embarrassment; the acquisition of a husband is the worthiest ambition a girl can have. No position carries with it more honor and more subsidiary rights than that of Wife and Mother.

Since he is so necessary an accessory, you cannot afford to give consideration to man's wishes. Willy-nilly he must be hunted down, nudged into a favorable position, and then pressured, bribed, needled, wheedled, teased, trapped, or if need be, tricked, into delivering himself body and bank-

8

book into your everlasting service. Do not be timid. Do not be squeamish. Your very life is at stake. Your social and economic status, your emotional well-being, your sexual salvation, your Motherhood potential—all are determined by marriage.

How deplorable that no effort is made to prepare the female for the most important project she will ever undertake, viz.:

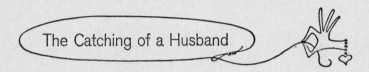

The Catching of a Husband

She is tossed out into the world, untutored and bewildered, and left to grope blindly in a highly competitive field.

It is my desire to do away with this hit-or-miss system. I have therefore written a practical manual filled with unscientific, factual, down-to-earth information, and I address it to all unmarried females who have passed their fifteenth birthday. No girl is too young to start working toward the ultimate goal, and none old enough to give up and retire from the contest.

You will find in these pages an analysis of the habits and weaknesses of the Male, a blueprint of his lairs and his secret paths, and a detailed description of the Methods—the 7 Lures, 5 Spellbinders, 8 Traps, 9 Formulas, and 4 Love Potions—by which he can best be taken. Equipped with this knowledge, you may go forth full of courage and zest, a happy huntress, ready for The Chase. And if he is elusive, this precious quarry you hope to carry home, do not throw away your weapons and cry out "I cannot! It is too difficult!" No living thing wants to be caught, not even a fly. Is it not natural that a thinking, reasoning man should employ all his ingenuity to remain free? You must be diligent in your efforts, obstinate in your determination. You must be willing to pursue him in far-off corners, fight off all rivals, and carry on dauntless in the face of impossible odds. For no effort is too great when the game you hunt is that most wanted, most useful, most valuable creature in the world—

A Husband

———◆——

THREE

Preparation for the Hunt

'Tis the motive exalts the action.
—M. J. PRESTON

Sedatives for the conscience

No GIRL SHOULD think of herself as sly and predatory, for
if she does she will somehow betray this fact and cause men
to flee from her in fright. Away with all feelings of guilt!
Believe wholeheartedly in the rightness, the nobility of your
quest!

Here are a few capsules for calming the uneasy conscience:

Capsule One. You are, it is true, a hunter. But your success
does not threaten the quarry with extinction; on the contrary, it guarantees its propagation. Furthermore, you do not
intend to devour him, but rather to make a pet of him.

11

Capsule Two. Although he does not always realize it,

☞ Every man needs a wife

He needs someone to cook for him, to take care of his laundry, to nurse his aches and pains, and to relieve his loneliness in the dark of night. The bachelor is plagued by the inefficiency and disinterest of the strangers who perform these services for him. Laundries lose his sox and crumple his collars, hospitals are indifferent to his sneezes, and he never knows when his light o'love is going to flit elsewhere. As to constant dining in restaurants, it is an act of mercy to rescue him from this dreary and expensive routine.

Capsule Three. It is not for practical purposes alone that a man needs a wife. He has also a profound Spiritual Need of marriage. Emile Durkheim, the renowned sociologist, has this to say about woman's role in matrimony: "... her devotion is indispensable to man to help him endure life."

Unfortunately, many a bachelor has not read Durkheim. In ignorance and fear he runs like a savage from the kind hands that offer him lifesaving serums. Like the savage, he must be persuaded that though the initial shock of the injection may be painful and is often followed by a lingering irritation, it is, in the end, good for him.

Verily, "... matrimony does woman less service than it does man ... it is he that profits more by it." * Remember these words. And while you are hot on the trail of your quarry, make this your hunting cry:

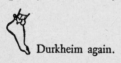

Durkheim again.

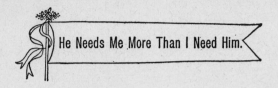

He Needs Me More Than I Need Him.

Tonics for the spirit

It is nice to know that in bringing man to the altar we are forcing life's dearest gifts on him. That we do so at no cost to ourselves, but rather at a considerable profit, is an added blessing.

Let us pause a moment in the privacy of these pages and take inspiration from the contemplation of

The 15 pleasures of wifehood

1. The pleasure of dependence

With what a carefree heart does a girl face the future, knowing that somone is legally and morally bound to provide her with bed and board and pay all her bills forevermore.

13

2. The pleasure of independence

Marriage brings release from the authority of parent and employer. A wife is gloriously free to do as she pleases, for a husband can neither fire her nor command her respectful obedience.

3. The pleasure of social prestige

The title MRS. standing in front of her name gives a girl status in society. It wins her the respect of thinking people everywhere, and enables her to look with condescension on all single females, though they be prettier, younger, smarter, or richer than she.

4. *The pleasure of retirement*

Home at last, the bride can throw away her calorie chart, high heels, girdles, and all the other uncomfortable accouterments of The Chase, and relax in an old bathrobe while she skins her catch.

5. *The pleasure of security*

Every girl who has ever worried about having a date for Saturday night or New Year's Eve, will appreciate the happy convenience of a permanent escort.

6. *The pleasure of the marital bed*

A man cannot run from his bed at night, but must lie still and listen while his wife delivers the lectures, complaints, and demands she has saved up for him during the day.

7. *The pleasure of free service*

How nice for a girl to have someone always on call to carry heavy things, repair whatever is broken, and unscrew tight lids.

8. *The pleasure of ownership*

Even if she marries a sailor or a traveling man, or a chronic absentee, a girl is glad to know that there is one male who, by contract, belongs to her and her alone.

9. *The pleasure of lazy leisure*

With a little ingenuity a wife can manage to sleep late, spend her afternoons at the movies, hide the dirty dishes in the oven, and at the same time convince her husband that woman's work is never done.

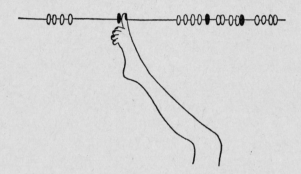

10· *The pleasure of innocent pleasure*

All the carnal delights forbidden a girl when she is single, become her sanctified duty when she is a wife.

11. *The pleasure of accomplishment*

A woman glows with pride when she sees the weekly income grow larger, and knows that it is her extravagance or greediness that is driving her husband on toward prosperity.

18

12. *The pleasure of giving orders*

It is customary for a wife to tell her husband what to wear, how to have his hair cut, what to do with his free time, how to conduct his business, how to spend his money, etcetera etcetera etcetera.

13. *The pleasure of motherhood*

No matter how silly she is, no matter how purple her past, a wife acquires wisdom and a shining halo the moment she becomes a Mother.

14. The pleasure of looking like a success

Regardless of whether she catches a miserable specimen or a prize, every bride gets the same golden band that proclaims her a success as a woman.

15. The pleasure of revenge

In a hundred subtle ways a wife can punish her husband for the trouble and pain he caused while she was trying to capture him. And she may also get even with any of his friends and relatives who pulled against her.

Do not expect to cram all 15 Pleasures into your marriage. Eight, even five, should suffice to make a girl happy. Indeed, there is so much joy to be had just from Pleasure No. ___ But enough! It is a waste of time to sit back and crow over the rewards that lie ahead. Let us, instead, attend to our knitting.

FOUR

Sex

BEFORE A GIRL can properly set about acquiring a husband she must become acquainted with some basic truths concerning Sex. Sex is an interesting subject. And a delicate one. I deplore the current tendency, fostered by our thought arbiters, to oversimplify and overpopularize it. They would have us believe that Sex is an ordinary, everyday fact of life, plain as an old shoe, with its feet planted solidly in biology.

Fiddle-dee-dee.

Sex is a variable—mystical, magical, symbolical, floating above the shifting sands of psychology. Among its mazes and its crazy-mirrors, where things are seldom what they seem, the Male himself is the most unreliable element of all. We will therefore begin our study with a peek behind his frontispiece.

The great male humbuggery

Let us examine the Male with clear, uncompromising eyes that are not fooled by bluff and sham. This is not to say that one should behave like the horrid little boy who blurted out, "But the Emperor wears no clothes!" I am not in favor of embarrassing Emperors and creating general dismay with an outcry against deception. How much happier everybody would have been if that child had whispered his observation in his mother's ear, or kept it to himself. One can maintain a diplomatic silence, and at the same time refuse to be deceived by a public conspiracy to pretend that something is what it is not.

Applying this to the matter at hand, consider the proposition that

☞ **Men are not as erotic as they claim (generally speaking)** ☜

One must grant there are exceptions. You cannot positively say of every male, as he swaggers about in full sexual regalia, that he is clothed in a fantasy. But you would do well to inspect him carefully and ask yourself if the medals he is wearing are fake and the banner he waves is false.

The fact is that men do not dare to be themselves. They are compelled to behave like satyrs. It is the fashion of the day to have a lusty, ostentatious appetite for Sex, and the man who has a small or refined or fluctuating one, hides the

fact scrupulously, claiming that his hunger is as big as, or bigger than anybody else's. If he did not do this he would be scorned. People would whisper, "... hormone deficiency" or "... psychiatric help" or "... queer bird" or "... something wrong there."

Because each man believes naively in the boasts of his fellows, and is unwilling to be different, he hesitates to admit even in his own heart that he does not measure up to the current heroic standards. As a result, every male, without exception, behaves as if he is deeply stirred by every attractive female, and has an appetite as wild and boundless as a stallion's. Now, you must know they cannot *all* feel that way *every* day, *every* night, *all* the time. It is a preposterous humbuggery.

We are not deceived by female padding. We do not accept as authentic every bosom that blossoms above a tiny waist. Let us look with similar skepticism upon the dashing figure cut by the male.

The bad effects of false padding

We have been told that our immediate ancestors suffered severe headaches because they were obliged to suppress their natural desires. But not a word is said of the harm done by today's insistence on Rabelaisian appetites, by the inflation of Sex's importance, and by the requirement that everyone maintain the same high intensity of wanting and having. Not all men are alike and it is really absurd that some should be made to feel apologetic simply because their lust is less lusty than others'.

The problem created thus for modern man is a serious one because it creates in turn a problem for woman. Since all men contrive to exhibit the same chic lustfulness, how can we guess what each one really wants? And if we do not know what he really wants, how are we to make him believe that we can give it to him?

There are no easy answers. But I have evolved a system for classifying men, and while it is neither simple nor perfect it does bring a degree of order to a seemingly hopeless mishmash.

Plumbing the male libido

Let us divide all men into categories A, B, C, D, E, F, G, H, I, J, K, L, M, N, and O. A represents the man with the greatest aptitude. O * is the man at the opposite end of the scale. The other letters represent the varying grades between the two extremes.

Actually this is a very coarse scale. To be accurate we should have to use the entire English alphabet, plus the Phoenician. However, so many letters would be cumbersome. For simplicity's sake we will work with this abbreviated group.

Study the letters for a while. Visualize them as men, each with his own particular endowments. After you have become familiar with them try to letter a man who interests you. This is not easy unless you have accumulated some revealing facts about him. Acceptable evidence can be obtained by:

1. Hearsay
2. Guesswork
3. Spying

Hearsay. Nothing that a man discloses about himself voluntarily, can be credited.

—If he ashamedly confesses he has been a libertine and a heartbreaker all his life—Do not believe him.

—If he hints or brags about his exploits—Do not believe him.

—If other men speak admiringly or indignantly of his conquests, you may assume they are repeating only what they heard from him—Do not believe them.

 Not to be mistaken for zero.

BUT

—If you get numerous first hand reports from ruined girls extolling his prowess ...

—If he is tearfully referred to in feminine circles as the Wild Bull of the Campus or the Galloping Goat of Beverly Hills—Then you may believe. He is an authentic Mr. A.

Guesswork

Example 1. A girl with strong intuitive powers may sense that her beau is not really subject to uncontrollable hunger every day in the week, but only on Tuesdays and Sunday afternoons. She has every right to guess he is an *H*.

Example 2. If a man is steadfastly decent, declining all intimate favors, if he frowns on other men's escapades, if he objects to chatting about erotic subjects, a girl may safely guess he is an *N* or *O*.

Example 3. A magnificent, muscled specimen of manhood is not necessarily a Mr. *A*, or *B*, or *C*, or even *G*. Nor is a skimpy scrap of a man necessarily a Mr. *N* or *O*. Nature is too coy to provide such obvious signs, and one can guess absolutely nothing from a man's appearance. Do not be misled by sheer bulk. Many a prize is concealed inside an insignificant package.

Spying. Immediately after learning a man's name, marital status, and occupation you should ascertain his normal temperature, pulse, and rate of respiration. This can be accomplished quite gracefully. Bring forth thermometer and stop watch and explain away your curiosity as a mere caprice.

Only a spiteful or excessively secretive man will refuse to divulge his temperature, pulse, etc. Most men will cooperate, which is fortunate, for without this information you can do no effective spying. You cannot, for instance, deduce that a man's heartbeat is suspiciously slow if you do not know its normal behavior.

A rudimentary exercise in spying

Lure the subject onto a dimly lit dance floor. While swaying to the music, stealthily work your thumb over to his wrist and place it on the pulse. When you have his count, slip the middle finger of your other hand down inside his collar and caress the back of his neck. Then very surreptitiously inch around toward his ear and tickle it with the forefinger. Now put your lips close to his other ear and murmur, "Mmmmmmm."

How much does his beat accelerate at each step of the investigation? Does it perhaps register no change? Does it slow down? Does it STOP!? Note the results and compare them with the readings you get each time the seductive cigarette girl crosses his line of vision.

While conducting these pulse tests you can check the rise and fall of his temperature by resting your cheek on his. No tricks are necessary in gauging his respiration, as this is a simple matter of looking and counting. (Even when kissing a man, a girl can always keep one eye open and watch him respire.) At the end of the evening, collate your facts properly and you will arrive at a rating.

You can devise any number of such examinations, using various kinds of stimuli. There are, alas, possibilities of error. It may well be that one has secured proof not of capability, but of excitability. A subject who displays all the symptoms of a Mr. A may actually be no more than a highly emotional Mr. M, while a genuine Mr. A may exhibit the imperturbability one expects of Mr. O: An overfed child does not always salivate at the sight of a sweet. Also, one sometimes gets conflicting results, or a skittish subject makes it difficult to take proper readings. As in all research, one is balked by the human factor.

By and large, however, if you conscientiously cross-check and coordinate the information gathered by means of Hearsay, Guesswork, and Spying, you should be able to classify your subject. A girl who even vaguely comprehends a man's sexual constitution has him in the classic position

for conquest. She will know approximately what to give and what to withhold and how and when, and he will be at her mercy.

But what is to be done when our sources fail us—when no rumors reach our ears, when we are given not the flimsiest clues on which to base our guesses, or when Spying produces a conclusion that contradicts Hearsay and confounds Guesswork?

The empiricist will say, "Oh the hell with it, I'm going straight to the fountainhead," and carrying the spirit of research to an extreme she deliberately gets to know her man far better than a girl has any right to know a man before she becomes his wife.

This is regrettable, for while Miss Know-It-All may learn the right answers, she commits the worst tactical error possible in the process. So eager is she to learn a man's letter, she foolishly does the very thing she would not do if she knew his letter in the first place. Thus she frustrates her own purpose. Far better to take your chances working in the dark than to rush down a well-lit path that leads straight to defeat.

How to muddle through in the dark

Do not be like Miss Know-It-All. The girl who gives herself away to an unlettered man is exposing herself to the most appalling dangers, the worst of which is that she may unwittingly give herself to a man who *does not really want her.*

Every day, all over the world, girls surrender themselves to seducers who are hoping to be rejected. These luckless men are astounded and chagrined by their ability to push over apparently strong walls. Still, having won a "Yes" they seldom run away, regardless of how inexperienced, inept, or scared they may be.

Why do these four-flushers beg for what they do not want? And why, in heaven's name, do they not retreat when threatened with success? They are like little boys who follow the big boys down to the swimming hole, doggedly determined to prove themselves. With their eyes shut tight, they grit their teeth and leap in, trusting that somehow they will not drown, that by some miracle they will suddenly be able to swim.

After floundering his way through a miserable seduction, Mr. M, N, or O will fold his tent and silently steal away— rarely, if ever, making a return appearance. If, on the other hand, his demands are refused, Mr. M, N, or O becomes a steadfast admirer. Though he shouts and pouts, he is happy beside a girl who lets him play Mr. A to his heart's content and never obliges him to prove himself. Entranced by her morality and nonviolent libido he is apt to become sincerly fond of her. Here we have the ideal conditions for luring a man into matrimony—propinquity, pleasure, and the absence of fear.

We see that by being too agreeable to a man from the latter part of the alphabet, a girl may lose a good prospect, and that, conversely, by preserving her chastity, whether real or assumed, she may increase her desirability in his eyes. For a low-letter man can be brought to the altar only by someone he believes is an ignorant virgin, a novice who is unable to make comparisons and must take him at his own evaluation.*

"But," you may object, "what if he is not Mr. O? Suppose he is Mr. A and he really and truly wants me?"

No matter. Strange as it may seem, the same incorruptible attitude gets the best results from one end of the alphabet to the other. And I must say, it is astonishing that anyone would even consider bestowing her favors on a Mr. A, or any other high-letter man. It indicates an overweening self-confidence, a readiness to rush in where angels fear to tread. A girl who has never skied does not plunge down a steep slope, a girl who has taken a few singing lessons does not give a recital. Why then should an amateur assume she is a fit vis-à-vis for a Mr. A, B, C, D, E, F, or G? Or H? How does she know she qualifies? Heaven is notably unjust in its distribution of gifts, and many are born without talent. Would it not be foolhardy to risk revealing to Mr. A that you have (1) No talent, or (2) A mediocre talent?

 Many a faithful wife is for this reason blissfully unaware all her life of what category her husband belongs in, or in fact that there is such a thing as categories.

How much less chancy it is to lead him on with little words and deeds that stimulate the imagination. Let him dream. Let him speculate. Let him believe that in your arms he will find the indescribable ecstacy sung by the poets plus the earthy delirium portrayed in the Italian cinema. It is not to your advantage to try to give him what he wants, but to make him think you have it to give.

Sexual compatibility

It is generally believed that in order to make a successful marriage, husband and wife must be sexually compatible. And how is this to be achieved? How is a girl to know when she has located a man she may marry with confidence? To date, but one method has been found—Trial and Error!

What a wicked idea this is. If a girl wants to match herself to a boy the way one matches colors, purple to purple, red to red, blue to blue, she may, before she has finished, have to test the whole spectrum. Not only does the procedure smack of looseness, it is extremely time-consuming. Many a timid girl, afraid of making a wrong choice, has wasted a good part of her youth conducting such a search.

But the saddest part of all is that the Trial and Error method is unreliable. It is unreliable for the following reasons:

1. In the wild confusion of an experiment one may be unable to distinguish colors; blues blend with purples and merge into reds, and it has been reported that some girls actually see rainbows.
2. These are not fast colors. Time and circumstance affect them. The participant who is a glowing pink today may next year be sere brown. Contrariwise,

an insipid green is often transformed into a flaming cerise.

3. Tests make people nervous, and in one of this nature where so much is at stake, either or both parties may fail to show their true coloring.

☞ **Do not take the compatibility test**

Even if it could accurately match up perfect pairs, I would be opposed to the test on the grounds that the men who most often suggest its use are rascals and deceivers. They are interested not so much in finding a life partner as in stealing unearned pleasures.

The variability of the male from A to O has been explored. The female needs no exploration. We each of us know what we are, I hope, and what we want, and what substitutions we are willing to accept. It would be folly to discuss such secrets in a book which may easily fall into the hands of men. Now then, based on what you know about the male and what you know about yourself, your inconsistencies, your dreams, your shortcomings, your phobias, your whims, and your adaptability, ask yourself what is the likelihood that you will capture a male who is ideal for your libido. Should the answer be "Precious little," do not give way to panic. Ask yourself, instead,

IS SEXUAL COMPATIBILITY QUITE QUITE NECESSARY?

I say No. It is a nice thing to have, but should be classed as a luxury rather than a necessity.

Would you hesitate to marry a man merely because he was not in perfect harmony with you regarding politics, religion, social problems, art, child-rearing, money-spending, or money-saving? Do you insist that your mentalities, personalities, and backgrounds be wholly compatible? Of course not—not if you ever expect to get married. Nowhere does one find perfection. It is unrealistic and unreasonable therefore to demand it in Sex.

Putting sex in its proper place

Sex is an integral part of married life, but considered timewise it is a very *small* part. Add up the number of waking hours in your week. There are about 112 if you are a good sleeper. Assuming that the husband you get goes to work, and that he spends time traveling to and from work, he will be absent from you, let us say, fifty hours in a week, which leaves sixty-two hours that you are free to spend with each other.* Estimate how many of those hours will be devoted to child care, eating together, watching TV, playing cards, conversing, quarreling, visiting, entertaining, reading, shopping, hobbying, etc., etc. Now estimate the number of hours you and your husband will spend in each other's embraces. Whether it is one quarter hour per week

 This should be a heartening figure to the girl who contemplates marrying a man she does not like very much. She can take further encouragement from the fact that many husbands are grateful if granted time off for masculine pursuits. There are women who manage to see their mates not more than 25 hours a week, of which less than 10 are spent without the presence of other people to relieve the dreadful aloneness. There are few fields of endeavor in which a woman can reap so many benefits from a 10-hour week.

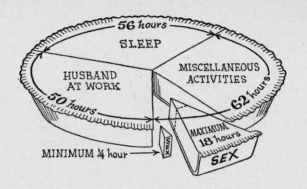

out of the sixty-two, or eighteen full hours * it is evident that Sex plays a relatively minor role in the week to week life of a married couple.

One should keep this in mind, and not lose perspective in viewing the various aspects of marriage. For instance, a far more serious threat than incompatibility is uncontrollable snoring. A husband who snores mercilessly, relentlessly, no matter how many times his wife pinches his nose, will destroy the peace of all her nights. And what happiness is there for a woman who can never get a good night's sleep? Likewise, marriage with a man who picks his teeth at the table will bring you a greater aggregate of aggravating hours than marriage to a man whose libido is not in line. So very much time is spent at the table.

To cite another example, take the girl who takes a husband who is without ambition, but whose libido is perfectly attuned to her own. The fleeting moments of rapture that are hers cannot balance out the hours spent gazing piteously at an empty garage, nor do they compensate for

 The latter is a rather optimistic figure selected to still the protests of braggarts.

the heartache of seeing other women in furs and jewels and cashmere sweaters.

While on the subject of time we should not forget that in marriage there is a sliding scale down which romantic love slips steadily as the years roll along. Nobody expects that a couple celebrating their twentieth anniversary will be as ardent as they were on their second. What of the thirtieth? And the fortieth? Do not be shortsighted. You are not getting married for a few passionate years, but for forever. You must plan for the long haul.

In conclusion

To a man Sex is more than just sex. It is a symbol. Through it he gives proof to the world and to himself that he is a MAN; he affirms his virility, his normality, and his everlasting youthfulness. Nothing can hurt his feelings more than the thinnest shadow of doubt about his sexual proficiency. He will better survive a slur on his ancestry or his honesty.

Therefore, never let a man suspect you are not quite sure whether he is Mr. *B* or Mr. *G* or Mr. *M*. Treat each one as if he is a certified Mr. *A*, and even Mr. *O* himself, ever eager to be deluded, will believe that it is so. If your eyes reflect the right image,* if he believes he is convincing one and all, strangers, friends, and sweethearts, that he is a Mr. *A*, that is enough to give a male supreme joy and self-confidence.

Ah, what power Sex has in the hands of a woman. How she can capture and enslave a man—not by exploiting her talents as a nymph, but by convincing him he is the satyr he longs to be.

 In the words of Virginia Woolf: "Women have served all these centuries as looking-glasses possessing the magic and delicious power of reflecting the figure of man at twice its natural size."

FIVE

Where to Look for Him

Go where the deer are playing, Hunter—
Fisher, go where the bass do bite—
Maiden, go where the men are fleeing,
And catch one in his flight.
— M. K. STRATFORD

THE MORE men a girl meets, the more chance there is she will come across ONE she can overpower. It is, therefore, of prime importance to

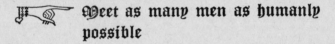 **Meet as many men as humanly possible**

The formula for accomplishing this is simple. In everything you do—in working, playing, worshipping, exercising, studying, shopping, vacationing, and convalescing, in the selection of a friend or a frock or a bus route or a dentist, waking and sleeping and daydreaming—keep your goal uppermost in mind, and make certain that everything you do will present you with the opportunity of meeting men.

38

So much for the future. One must also cast a critical eye on what has gone before. A girl who has allowed herself to be tissed and tossed about by fortune, who has planned carelessly or not at all, is bound to be in a losing position. She can hardly hope to succeed without correcting the mistakes of the past. This may mean altering a small detail in her way of life, or it may mean a complete upheaval—a throwing overboard of home, country, loved ones, and ideals. Drastic measures, yes, but when things are in a mess, revolution is the classic solution.

That there are a few somber elements involved in this project cannot be denied, but on the whole it should be fun if approached in a spirit of wholesome gaiety.

The Ways and Means of collecting men are many. I shall analyze here all the aspects of life and living as they affect The Search—i.e., Geographic Location, Education, Careers, Friends, Vacations, Pastimes, and so forth.

Geographic location

Our great country, so rich in other natural resources, is short of approximately 2½ million men. This is deplorable but it does not mean—as some alarmists believe—that 2½ million of our girls are, as a consequence, doomed to be spinsters. For many of these excess girls have already been wed and widowed. Moreover, panicky observers ought to be reminded that some of the men we do have can be used more than once. Indeed we may safely estimate that four men can marry five women—and often do. This is possible in our monogamous society because one out of every four marriages ends in divorce, throwing 25 per cent of all married men back into the reservoir of free males, and making them available as mates for the surplus women.

39

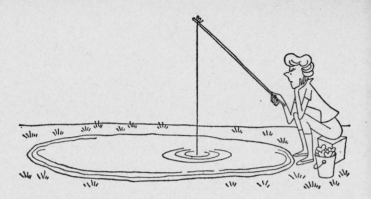

Obviously, the much advertised shortage of 2½ million men is a figure and not a fact.

What does concern us is that the male population is very unevenly—one might say haphazardly—distributed throughout the nation. A girl should ask herself not "Are there enough single men in my country?" but "Am I in the section of my country where there are enough single men?"

It is a rare spinster who knows the facts about the sex ratio in her region. Fortunately, your government stands ready to supply these figures for the small sum of 60 cents. Send your remittance to the Department of Commerce, Bureau of the Census, Washington 25, D.C. and ask for pamphlet PC(1) 1B of the 1960 Census Summary. Study the tables earnestly. Then ask yourself this vital question:

> Am I living in an area that is adequately stocked with men, or do the unmarried females outnumber the unmarried males?

The importance of a favorable ratio is inestimable. Let me demonstrate:

If 100 beautiful, charming, wealthy girls are isolated on Island A, which is inhabited by 90 men, it must follow that 10 of these girls, no matter how adorable, will remain unmated (if monogamy prevails).

On the other hand, if 90 girls, all plain, disagreeable and penniless, are isolated on Island B, which is inhabited by 100 men, every girl will acquire a mate with the greatest of ease (if monogamy prevails).

Concealed in this little parable is a valuable lesson: A girl's chances are determined not so much by *what* she is, as *where* she is.

Regardless of her assets, she is seriously handicapped if she is living in a place that has a surplus of women. Firstly, a definite number of females in her region are doomed to remain husbandless, and she may be one of them. Secondly, men, when they are a scarce commodity, become spoiled, capricious, and most difficult to yoke. Thirdly, unnerved by the pressure of competition, a girl cannot pick and choose, but seizes on the first willing man that comes to hand.

What is to be done to surmount these conditions? Let us return to the Islands for a solution. If A and B were not totally isolated, what action would you advise for the ten extra girls on Island A? Would you suggest they sit by and wait until divorce frees a man for remarriage? Or would you tell them to flee to Island B, where they could avail themselves of the ten leftover men?

The same sensible advice applies to every girl who finds herself in a similar pickle.

𝔇o not remain where women outnumber men

Pack your suitcase (or your trunk) and Go! Run! Fly! Though it be painful to leave one's home in a beautiful and exciting place like, let us say, Washington, D.C., to

move to a remote backwater like, let us say, Lawton, Oklahoma, anyone who is serious about finding a husband will not permit sentiment or aesthetic considerations to hold her back.

Lawton is cited advisedly, for there you will find 100 males for every 71 females! * Our great capitol city, on the other hand, is so hopelessly undermanned, that if every bachelor inside its boundaries were forced to wed tomorrow, there would be tens of thousands of girls left without partners.

A deficiency of single men is the greatest evil that exists in our big cities. Even New York, queen of them all, rich and proud and peerless, has a meager supply, with only 88 males to every 100 females. This is a surprise to some people, who think that you can find everything in a large metropolis.

The census reports are full of surprises. One would hardly suspect for example, that the gigantic, virile state of Texas which seems the very synthesis of maleness, is more feminine than masculine in its population. Still, Texas has a kind of irresistible lure—no doubt because of all those oil wells—and the girl who really wants to go there should not be discouraged by the general picture. A perusal of the statistics † will reveal that individual places within the state have an excellent sex ratio. Recommended are Wichita Falls, El Paso, and Amarillo. Dallas, sad to say, is ill-provided, and Corpus Christi is not much better.

 All sex ratio figures given herein apply to population over the age of eighteen.

 Check and prove all figures, even mine, writing to the local Chamber of Commerce for verification.

We find this divergence in every one of the states—some cities are poor in men, others rich. The timid maid who shudders at the prospect of going far from home can take heart from these intrastate differences. If you live in male-poor Savannah, you need not leave your beloved Georgia. A short trip will take you to Columbus where there is an abundance of men. A little enterprise spells the difference between marriage and spinsterhood, success and failure. The girls of Richmond, Virginia, for instance, who languish without suitors the year around, must be marked 'lazy,' for no more than 95 miles away, in their own state, lies Norfolk which boasts 117 men to every 100 women!

While a girl ought lose no time in fleeing a barren region, she cannot afford to be careless in choosing her destination. Particular attention should be given to cities with identical names. These can be confusing and have been the cause of serious disappointments. Only last year a Boston lass left the Massachusetts wasteland (88 males to every 100 females) in such haste that she accidentally bought a ticket for Jackson, Miss. instead of Jackson, Mich. Though Miss. and Mich. are somewhat similar when read casually, there is a vast difference between their Jacksons. The one in Mississippi is probably the worst place in the whole United States so far as sex ratio is concerned, whereas the one in Michigan, where the emigrant from Boston meant to go, has an attractively balanced population— 106½ men to every 100 women. She did not discover her mistake until six months later when, becoming suspicious, she had the good sense to reexamine her census tables.

A thorough investigation of the census is very reward-ing.* One should be acquainted with the figures on cities

* Atlantic City is an anomaly. According to the 1960 Census it has only 86 males to 100 females. But oh, what a harvest is to be reaped

44

both near and far, including those of foreign lands. A girl with vision may see the wisdom of forsaking not only her State, but her Country, and even the Temperate Zone, in order to relocate where the sex ratio is most favorable to her. Opportunities abound in distant places like Alaska and Australia, to name just a few at the beginning of the alphabet.

And let us not neglect to explore the possibilities offered by our friendly neighbor, Canada. I knew a long bony girl who lived quietly with her family in sunny Pasadena,* unnoticed, uncourted, unloved. At thirty, in a mood of desperation, she migrated to a dreary city in Canada, where she settled in a miserable boarding house and took a mundane job. Despite these stark conditions, her life was like a young girl's dream of heaven, due to the presence of an excessive number of males in the territory. At dances she danced every dance, for in this wonderland the walls were lined only by men; at church, kind masculine hands helped turn the pages of her prayerbook, and always there was someone to escort her home; and at the table in her boarding house, men vied for the privilege of passing her the ketchup.

Within a year the happy immigrant was married to a touring bachelor, who gratefully wrapped her in muskrat and mushed off with her to his ranch in northern Manitoba.

"Ooh," you may exclaim, "it's much too cold up there."

True. But one cannot boggle at the weather when one's future hangs in the balance. Ask yourself this: Which

---

here. For this is the city of conventions. A never-ending stream of professional and business men pours into its hotels all the year round, providing a floating male population which is enormous and uncounted.

Stay away from Pasadena. There we find a most distressing situation —78 males to every 100 females. One wonders at parents who choose to raise daughters in such an environment.

would I rather be, a sunbaked spinster lolling on the sands of Long Beach, or a cherished, if chilblained wife, watching the aurora borealis over the Arctic Circle?

Hardship accompanies every pioneering effort. Let us remember our heritage. Our forebears crossed an unfriendly ocean to settle in a wilderness; they froze and starved and forfeited their scalps in order to achieve their goal. Surely the daughters of such a people will not hesitate to uproot themselves to go in search of their heart's desire.

Careers

Almost everybody works at something—either to make the time pass by, or to acquire prestige, or simply to earn a living. If you are an unmarried female these are not sound reasons. They will mislead you into focusing your interest on salary, working conditions, pensions, fun, intellectual fulfillment, or fame, when you should be thinking of your work in terms of men. How many men and what kind of men will you meet—that is what counts. For no career can offer the benefits that go with marriage, and it is very short-sighted indeed to measure a job by any

yardstick other than its mating potential.

Many intelligent girls do not know how to appraise a job. A high percentage failed to give the correct answer to the following question. Study it and test your own ability to make an evaluation.

Question—Which of these two situations do you consider more desirable?

1. Stenographer in the busy sales office of a large typewriter company. Salary is $55, the hours are long, and you are required to turn in the stub of your old pencil before you may have a new one. Your desk, a center of noisy activity, is constantly surrounded by salesmen clamoring for your services.
2. Secretary to an elderly historian (married) who pays $90 a week, and never notices the hours you keep, who provides a cushion for your chair, carpeting for your feet, and does not care how much postage and stationery you take home.

If you do not choose Situation #1 at once, if you linger even briefly over the goodies listed in #2, you are not thinking properly. Superficial trimmings blind you to the true worth of a position.

Look about with sharp-eyed awareness, and choose the right job. And if you have already chosen a wrong one, do not tarry there, but find something else at once.

For some it is not merely a question of changing to the right job. I speak of those hapless maidens who are wasting away in the wrong career. If you have blundered thus and find that you come in contact with women and children only, or with nobody at all, you must change your career, regardless of the trouble involved. You are tilling in a desert while fertile lands lie waiting on all sides.

Obviously a beautician, poetess, masseuse, milliner, kindergarten teacher, or corsetiere will not fare as well as a waitress, a nurse, an actress, a chemist, an airline hostess, reporter, athlete, salesgirl, photographer, or palmist.

My cousin Susannah made a bad start when she thoughtlessly became a serious painter. For several years she worked alone in her charming studio in New Orleans, meeting only with mediocre success and a few art dealers, until, on the advice of a wise old fortune-teller she gave it up. Deserting her ivory tower, she went to work for a man (unmarried) who manufactured wallpaper. She was obliged to create hideous designs and do odd jobs, such as filing papers and typing bills and dusting the samples—all this in a crowded little office she shared with her boss. So crowded was it, that the busy wallpaper man was forever squeezing past Susannah as he moved about the room, or being butted by her when she bent over the files.

But it was this very cramped condition that resulted in a glorious denouement, for one day as he tried to dash past her the two of them became wedged between his desk and the wall. Caught thus, he was unable to avoid embracing her. One embrace led to another, and soon they were kissing and fondling, and fondling and kissing. This sort of thing, once begun, rapidly becomes habit, and in order to restore order in his office, the wallpaper man decided to marry Susannah and keep her at home.

Susannah's experience vividly illustrates the old axiom—

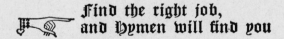 **Find the right job, and Hymen will find you**

49

Friendship

Ovid said, "The common man values friendships for their utility." This is as true in our day as it was in his, and when a concept remains unchanged through the centuries we can be sure it is a sensible one.

Look about you, and with your goal in mind, select the proper friends. Most valuable is—

The Well-Connected Girl. Some girls have brothers and cousins and young uncles. In their homes the kitchens are cluttered with snacking men, the living rooms are livened by hearty voices discussing electric razors and carburetors. Moustaches and pipes and trousered legs everywhere delight the eye, and the frequent slamming of doors and tramp of big feet advertise the presence of the male.

Other girls live in houses inhabited only by mothers, sisters, and aunts—and fathers who respect the quiet of a tidy feminine household.

Can there be any doubt as to which class of girl is more desirable? Yet most friendships are formed without looking into family connections. Ask the nearest girl why she chose her dearest friend and the reply will be, "She has a car," or "She lives conveniently nearby," or "She forced herself on me."

As for the sentimentalist who holds that friendship should be motivated by affection, there is no reason why she cannot grow fond of a girl richly endowed with male relatives.

Also recommended for friendship is—

The Popular Girl. The girl who is beautiful or wealthy or has some other attribute that causes male admirers to crowd around her. Here again one gains constant access to a pool of men. Many must of necessity be neglected by the Popular Girl and if you are alert you should be able to siphon off at least one reject for yourself.

Do not slight—

Neighbors, Parents' Cronies, and other Assorted Folk. Those who are mature, appreciate the attention of younger people. By endearing yourself to the parents and grandparents of marriageable males, you can gladden old hearts while promoting your personal interests. More than one son has been served up at the altar by his own mother.

There is hardly a person in this world who is not worthy of our friendship. Indeed, to be truly Christian, we should love everyone. It follows, then, that wherever we bestow our friendship it is well placed, and if this is so, you can in all good conscience select for your intimates those who can be of use to you.

Vacation and travel

It seems an excellent idea to use one's vacation to go off on a cruise or to a popular resort in search of a husband. Indeed, the idea is so obvious that everybody does it, and as a result the vacation paradise * is invariably overpopulated by eager females.

What can be expected by the vacationing girl when she is faced with

a) men made cocky by their scarcity?
b) a carnival atmosphere of infectious *laissez faire?*

There is small chance she will be able to annex a husband under these conditions.

The above statement will no doubt be greeted by cries of "Well, Betsy (or Mary or Barbara) got hers that way!"

Did she? Lucky girl. My statistics prove that only 1½ girls out of 73 achieve their goals while thus handicapped.

Certainly there are a few successes. An impressionable lad, scorched by moonlight, inflamed by perfume, overcome by a tumultuous pulse, may impulsively plight his troth, thinking to perpetuate the magic of the moment in matrimony. It also sometimes happens that a hung-over man, clinging to the wall of a social hall, may clutch a leftover girl for support, and finding it is much easier to stand in this manner, will be unwilling to let go. And there are a number of other odd quirks of happenstance which can result in a winning combination. But a thrifty girl will not

I use "paradise" in the Ancient Persian sense, i.e., a hunting park.

squander her hopes, her savings, and her precious fortnight to go where the odds are against her, 73 to 1½.

Instead she will select a place that attracts many men and few women.

—A rustic spot noted for good fishing or hunting.
—The locale of an extended sporting event—a golf tourney, horse show, regatta, car races, tennis matches, etc., etc.
—A college town overflowing with professors, tutors, and students.
—The hotel where a convention is scheduled for philatelists, spiritualists, physicists, dentists, taxidermists, engineers, financiers, educators, exterminators, aviators, decorators, statisticians, politicians, magicians, morticians, or whatever.

It should be possible for an energetic girl to cover four different events during a two-week vacation. The notices that appear in newspapers, sports magazines, and trade journals furnish complete information about the byways and hideaways where men congregate. Follow them—for it is precisely at a time when they are engrossed in their own pursuits that men are likely to be caught unaware.

The matchmaker

While millions of maidens are trying to flush out suitable mates from the jumbled mass of the general population, thousands of others tiptoe secretly to a Marriage Broker's office for theirs. Here, neatly arranged in file drawers, labeled and cross-indexed, is a stock of eligible men. A girl need waste no time rummaging in a grab bag of unsorted material—men already married, men who do not want to marry, men who are too young or too old or

53

too much this or too little that. In the broker's office, order and efficiency prevail.

You would like a husband in his thirties? Someone who is fond of tennis and children and fast cars? Republican, a pharmacist, tall, with blue eyes and a sense of humor? The broker's hand darts straight to the file where men in their thirties are kept; she riffles through them and picks out one. "Sorry," she shakes her head after a moment. "His eyes are brown and his game is golf. See me next week. We always have something new coming in."

Although the broker cannot make a man to your order, she does weed out the undesirables and you can at the very least count on meeting someone who is genuinely interested in marriage—for these men, you understand, pay out a sum of money, just as you do, for the privilege of being registered in the matrimonial bureau.

The fee is reasonable for the service rendered and usually buys one year's worth of introductions. If no match is made in that time, a hopeful client will subscribe for another year. A broker told me of a young woman who became what might be described as a compulsive subscriber, addicted to the service. Like a gambler showing up at the five-dollar window at Belmont after every race, she would appear at the broker's office the day after her subscription ran out, take a deep breath, count out the required sum, and cry, "I'll take another year's worth!" This continued for five years, during which time the insatiable girl ran through hundreds of candidates without settling on a husband. Whenever she met someone nice she thought, What if the next one is nicer? Furthermore, so delightful did she find it to have a date with a new man every week, that she was loath to exchange the excitement of numbers and variety for the monotony of monogamy.

Finally, one day, realizing that she was becoming spoiled by the gay life she purchased from the matrimonial bureau, she decided to break the habit. She picked up a card that had fallen out of the broker's files and said, "Miss Brooks, whatever he is, I'll take him." And over the protests of the conscientious Miss Brooks, she did, although the man came out of the wrong drawer, and was not the age, size, or type she had specified.

Hers was an unusual case. Many girls obtain husbands in their first year with a Marriage Broker. Others are disappointed and drop out, having gained nothing but a number of dates for their money. Some, out of an exaggerated sense of economy, accept a husband who is not exactly what they want, rather than lose their investment. But all in all, the employment of a broker is a most practical way to seek a husband.

I have often thought how lovely it would be if we had a government agency to manage the important business of introducing the right boys to the right girls. With a well-trained staff, and a huge file containing detailed information on all unmarried persons, it would be a fairly simple matter to set up a rotating system for providing our girls with appropriate candidates. Every girl would meet a limitless number of graded men, and never would she be placed in the undignified position of having to go out and find them for herself.

The merits of such an arrangement would be so apparent that the public would forget its current prejudice against matrimonial bureaus. Applicants would approach its doors squarely rather than crabwise, and speak without embarrassment of the place where they found their mates. There would, no doubt, be some abuses, as in all government projects. High officials would snatch up all the plums for their own daughters, sisters, and aunts. But this is a custom as ancient as making matches and should not discourage us from promoting the scheme. The important thing is that it puts marriage within the reach of everyone, and reduces to a minimum the amount of effort that need be expended. Let us hope that we will have socialized courtship within the near future. I urge each and every one of you to write to your Congressman. It is a cause worth fighting for.

The amateur matchmaker

Unofficial, unpaid—the Amateur Matchmaker operates on her own initiative, and can be found everywhere and anywhere. A neighbor, a relative, a friend, a chance acquaintance may be your destined Cupid. Do not stamp her "Busybody" and "Meddler." Although she may be either or both of these, she is also often a romantic do-gooder.

A neighbor of mine has eight children, aged eighteen and seventeen, fourteen and thirteen, ten and nine, six and five. She has two dogs, two cats, two birds, two goldfish, two maids. She has a passion for pairs and actually runs a fever when she loses one glove or one earring. This symmetrical-minded woman cannot rest happily until she has found a partner for every single creature or thing she sees. As you may have guessed, no unmarried girl or man who crosses her path escapes from her determined efforts to make couples out of singletons. This odd tic has resulted in a number of marriages.

Whatever it is that motivates the Amateur Matchmaker, scorn her not. She may strike upon just the match for you.

Education

An investment in knowledge pays the best interest.
—BEN FRANKLIN

Fortunate is the girl who is enrolled at a coeducational college or university. This is the place and these are the years when a girl can snap up a boy with a simple twist of his wrist.

It is just when young men are supposed to be concentrating on their studies that they are most likely to be dreaming of girls, and cutting out photos of beauties in bikinis. How vulnerable they are, how impressionable, how unafraid, how full of passion. What perfect hothouse conditions for the forced flowering of desire into marriage!

Educators are aware of all this and do what they can to foster it, for they are deeply concerned with preparing the young for happy, useful lives. This is true the world over, even in staid old England. Only recently the girls at Oxford were notified a full hour had been added to the period devoted each evening to entertaining friends of the opposite sex.

Mothers and fathers, less astute than educators, sometimes think that learning is the be-all and the end-all. They insist on sending their girls to female schools, failing to realize that such an institution is no better than a squirrel cage unless closely connected with a school for men.

Parents who want their daughter to squeeze the greatest value out of her school years will not only agree to sending her to a coeducational institution, they will help her to select one with the best Male/Female ratio. They will go further. They will give her strong guidance in selecting her major. It would of course be cruel to flatly rule out Journalism or Home Economics or Education. But a girl who is smart enough to get into college can be reasoned with, and if her parents tell her that in a typical year 6,339 Males and 44,707 Females earned their B.A.'s in General Teaching Fields, she might be persuaded to consider a more rewarding major. In Architecture, for example, during that same typical year, only 74 Females were graduated in the company of 1,639 Males. In Accounting, 10,718 Males with 498 Females! In Law, 9,661 Males with 264 Females!! In Forestry, 1,344 Males with 2 Females!!!

These and related figures can be found in a book entitled *Statistical Abstract of the U.S.* Sponsored by the United States Department of Commerce, it is a thoroughly reliable publication and is recommended reading for every mother who has a daughter of school age.

A student who has solved her most pressing problem, who knows where her wedding ring is coming from, has peace of mind and can apply herself unstintingly to earning

58

high grades and honors. It is my hope that the segregated girls' schools will eventually be outlawed, for when coeducation becomes compulsory, we will in one fell swoop raise to a splendid new peak both the marriage rate and our scholastic standards.

Adult education

No matter what your schooling has been, you can benefit by further study. Broaden your horizons. Take a course in carpentry, in navigation, in political science, radio transmission, aviation, astronomy, or automobile engines. Dreary though these subjects may seem, they are the very ones that interest men, and there will be few females among your classmates.

Always be the first to arrive at class. Then you can shift your location from place to place as the room fills up, until you are next to the most likely looking male. When class is over, linger near the exit. You may be able to attach yourself to someone as he leaves, or tag along with a group going out for coffee. (Once you are seated in the coffee shop, each man will assume you were invited by one of the others.) Do not overlook your unmarried male teachers. They are stationary targets, always available for conferences, and no less vulnerable to flattery and gifts than other men are.

The utmost subtlety should be exercised in making overtures to teacher or fellow students. A lost shoe, a fancied mouse, a coughing spell—only genteel attention getters are acceptable. The halls of learning are, after all, not an amusement park, and one must conduct oneself with fitting restraint.

59

Pastimes

The way a girl spends her leisure time is an index to her character.

Does she like to stay at home with a good book? *She is lazy.* Is she addicted to sewing, weaving, knitting? *She is an escapist.* Has she a host of female friends always ready for cards, chatting, watching TV? *She is a coward.* Does she write poetry? *Hoity-toity!*

Girls with these bad traits are unlikely to find husbands. One must be industrious, rugged, dauntless, and democratic. Pastimes should be chosen not with frivolous pleasure in mind but with an eye to the Main Chance.

Politics is a nice pastime provided one is careful not to become involved in anything nasty. Keep your attention on the energetic young men who make this field so attractive, and let the issues take care of themselves. You cannot marry an issue.

I put this rather strongly because of a deplorable incident in which a relative of mine opposed an admirer, a rich young Reactionary, on the subject of nuclear tests. Her stand had absolutely no effect on global decisions and resulted only in her losing a prospective mate. This headstrong girl had made an identical blunder a few years earlier when she became so overwrought while defending Eisenhower's paintings that she shouted, "Pinko!" at the rich young Liberal who attacked them, thus creating a rift that never healed.

If, like my relative, you cannot refrain from having opinions, stay out of politics. Go in for something less controversial, such as

Sports—a pastime which enables you to build up your muscles and your marriage chances at the same time and puts no strain on the emotions. It is not necessary to excel at anything. What is important is that you show yourself off to advantage. Select your sport according to the costume that goes with it. For example, if your legs are lovely, swim or play tennis. (If you are knock-kneed you will look better mounted on a horse or a bicycle.)

Should you engage in a strenuous sport, do not exert yourself and become perspired and rumpled. A few minutes of activity is sufficient and if you really do not like athletics you can simply stroll about or lounge on the sidelines, looking friendly. Nobody will notice you are not actually participating.

Do not avoid crowds. Find a place that is well patronized by men, and appear there at established intervals. Loyalty to a particular place and even to a particular day and hour will make you a "regular" and you will get to know the other regulars.

The best sports are "group sports" such as hiking, hosteling,* mountain climbing, and fox hunting. On a trip with the Appalachian Mountain Club (three weeks of white-water canoeing) I saw a couple meet and plight their troth before they reached civilization. A man is forced to look for all sorts of possibilities in a girl when he is thrown into her company day after day, night after night.

I cannot stress too much the advantage of coming into contact wth the same man over and over again under informal conditions. His odd physique, his pointed ear, his funny tooth, his hairy back—these lose their strangeness with repeated viewing. Similarly your own flaws become familiar and, eventually, not noteworthy. Friendships that would never result from a single meeting, frequently blossom when two people have the opportunity to recover from the shock of the first encounter.

Hobbies are good because hobbyists of a kind tend to gather in closely knit cliques. Sympathy and trust are bound to prevail among people united by a common interest, particularly one that is ridiculed or misunderstood by the uninitiated. It is not surprising, therefore, that Romance is rampant in the clubs formed by stamp collectors, chicken fanciers, nudists, dahlia breeders, gourmets, health faddists, etc., etc., ad infinitum.

Even the girl who lives in a remote village can reach out and make rewarding connections, for Hobbyists have

 A wonderful world is open to the girl who owns a bicycle. She can spend weeks or weekends roaming the countryside on it, accompanied by robust young men and certified chaperones—all provided by American Youth Hostels Inc. For literature send to national executive office, 14 West 8th Street, New York City.

friendly little periodicals which serve to put their far flung ilk in touch with each other. An exchange of information and material through the mail promotes a hearty camaraderie that transcends political differences and national boundaries.

I recently read about the case of a young Daughter of the American Revolution, Mississippi Chapter, who traded rocks with a Yankee integrationist. Out of this mineralistic correspondence there developed a friendship that progressed from an exchange of rocks to an exchange of portraits, and then compliments, and finally, marriage vows.

Music offers much in all its forms of expression—duets, quartets, bands, symphony orchestras, choral societies, opera groups. Duets are a little dangerous—every note you play is clearly heard and if you are not precise you are more likely to infuriate your partner than win him. In a quartet, which invariably takes itself more seriously than a duet, the danger is even greater. Unless you are quite sure of your musicianship, it is better to hide away in the safety of a larger company. Amateur symphony orchestras are lovely and predominantly male. The lone female sitting in a forest of dinner jackets has the same compelling appeal as a girl in a man's army.

If you like to sing, attach yourself to an Opera Group. Hardly an opera written does not highlight the Male/Female relationship. The baritone and the tenor are forever fighting each other for the soprano, two lovers inevitably join in a duet to swear eternal love, there is always a passionate aria to be sung by a love-sick hero—all of which tends to charge the atmosphere with the kind of emotion that breeds matrimony. In short, singing is a top-notch hobby—and you need not let an inferior voice deter you, for singers are always complaining of being in bad voice and you may get months of valuable work done before it is discovered that you never are in good voice.

Entertainment. If you enjoy the theater, the opera, the ballet, or symphony concerts, and no one invites you to go, go nevertheless. But go by yourself. You may attract the attention of a lonely man who would never approach you if you had a companion. Two girls, giggling and chatting and lighting each other's cigarettes during the intermission, present a formidable picture to a man unless he is quite brash. And no one wants to make the acquaintance of a brash man without a formal introduction.

In striking up a friendship with any stranger, there is an element of danger. Even a quiet, shy fellow may prove to be a murderer. But criminal records indicate that a girl is just as likely to be murdered by her husband, her fiancé, her married lover, her rejected suitor, or a passing gunman, as by a stranger she has picked up at a Lawrence Welk broadcast.

I, for one, do not share the common prejudice against unconventional meetings, perhaps because my own parents met without formal introduction. By a stroke of luck it happened that their subscription seats for the Philharmonic adjoined one another. After sitting side by side on alternate Mondays with no more than an exchange of polite nods, through a season of Beethoven, Brahms, and Mahler, they were overcome one night by the Liebestod, impulsively clasped hands, left at the intermission, and by midnight were solemnly betrothed.

There are some who will say, "Lucky for your mother that your father was not a homicidal maniac." How true. But, then, a girl can hardly move about without taking risks of one sort or another. The man you meet at a party or on a cruise is rarely presented to you along with a dossier on his character, past history, and mental stability. Blind faith must guide us in appraising new friends.

SIX

The Dikdook

It is a common enough experience for a girl to appear in a public place, well dressed, eager, and bubbling with gaiety, only to be completely ignored. Sometimes she has to pinch a passerby to prove to herself that she is actually there. Why does she blend into the background? Why is she an indistinguishable blob? Sadly she concludes that a vital ingredient is lacking in her appearance or personality.

In truth what is lacking is *something* that will put a flattering spotlight on her, *something* that will turn all eyes in her direction,* *something* that will ignite spontane-

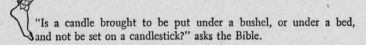

"Is a candle brought to be put under a bushel, or under a bed, and not be set on a candlestick?" asks the Bible.

ous conversations and instantaneous friendships. This *something* I call for clarity's sake, a *dikdook*.

A girl cannot have too many dikdooks. A dikdook can be small, ring in your nose for instance, or a dikdook can be fairly sizable, as an old lady in a wheel chair.

Of what possible use is an old lady in a wheel chair, you may ask. Of incalculable use! Nothing wins more kindly smiles, admiring glances, offers of help, and friendly overtures than a girl pushing such a dikdook. In railroad stations, in the street, in trains, theaters, restaurants, and hotel lobbies, her coming and going evokes the attention usually accorded a celebrity.

The girl with the Old Lady in a Wheel Chair not only attracts attention, she inspires the tenderest sentiments in that very sentimental creature, Man. Who can resist her?

If you take an Old Lady for a dikdook, you should quickly let it be known that she is simply a guest you have invited along on your vacation or for a one-day excursion,

whichever the case may be. This will remove any fear that you are permanently burdened by a troublesome dependent, and indicate that you are an angel of goodness who voluntarily devotes her leisure time to making an Old Lady happy.

You should have no difficulty in persuading an Old Lady in a Wheel Chair to be your guest companion. If, however, you do not know such a person, you might apply to an institution that houses aged people and it is quite possible they will lend you one of their ladies.

I might say in passing, that if you are unable to borrow an Old Lady in a Wheel Chair, an Old Lady with a Cane is also very good. And even without a cane, any really old Old Lady is a dikdook par excellence.

Not nearly as effective but still not to be overlooked as a dikdook, is the Dear Little Child with an outgoing personality. Such a one can be relied upon to make friends wherever you go and will bring you the same kind of favorable attention as an Old Lady, though to a far lesser degree. It should be trained to address you distinctly as Sis or Aunt So-and-so, thereby serving notice that you are not its mother.

If you do not have a little sister, brother, niece, nephew, or cousin, and must borrow one outside the family, be sure you know its habits. A companion who has temper tantrums, or a queasy stomach, or sudden attacks of homesickness, or one who will not respect your authority, can turn a holiday into a nightmare. On the other hand, a civilized little creature who can be trained to display a flattering fondness for you, is a veritable treasure.

However, even at its best, this dikdook has certain drawbacks. It cannot be tucked into bed and left alone at night like an Old Lady. One either retires early, losing the evening hours, or one must find a reliable nursemaid to leave with it. It cannot be taken to cocktail lounges or other interesting haunts, whereas an Old Lady can be wheeled anywhere, and may even be your passport to some rather questionable places.

I am tempted to say that it is better to restrict the use of a child companion to one day excursions. But so many victories have been reported by girls who took along a little boy or girl on vacation, that I hesitate to advise against it. And in this respect, it has been noted that an underprivileged child wins for his hostess five times as many admirers as an ordinary child—so deeply moved are men by an act of kindness.

A word of caution: Never take a child to a locale where there are other children. One child in a world of adults can be enchanting, an adorable little plaything, full of surprises and cute sayings. But children in quantity are unbearable. Noisy, quarrelsome, demanding, they inspire every adult with a desire to smack them. In such circumstances your dikdook is a drag.

Dogs are often as bright and friendly as the best child, and can serve the same purpose. Many people prefer a dog. A well-behaved one requires a minimum of care—no teeth-brushing, bathing, dressing, undressing, redressing, and it does not have to be entertained.

Much can be said for a good dog, either as a temporary or permanent confederate. In a charmingly uninhibited way he considers everybody his friend, and his friends become your friends. No man is too shy or too aloof to respond to the overtures of a dog, and hardly ever is one mean enough to snub him. That is why you never see The Girl With a Dog standing neglected on the sidelines. She is sure to meet everybody.

If you are not a dog lover, try to find some other kind of

animal to share your affections and your holiday. Cats, monkeys, falcons, lambs, cheetahs—all these have been used effectively. Fish are utterly useless companions. Birds are quaint but appealing. A nondescript female who carries a warbler in a cage will not pass unnoticed. Gallant men will assist her on every side, move her luggage, help her get water or bird seed, protest the objections of conductors, ushers, or room clerks, and offer protection from drafts. And how they will admire this girl who is so sweet, so soft-hearted, she could not bear to leave her little pet behind.

You will observe that all the dikdooks described in the preceding pages have three points in common—

1. Each one attracts attention.
2. Each one provides an easy introduction to strangers.
3. Each one puts the user in a flattering light.

Such dikdooks are the best and with a little effort one can discover or create others of the same type.

However, there are excellent dikdooks which do not possess all three advantages. For example, crutches. If you have had several disappointing vacations, why not try one on crutches? They can be rented at reasonable rates, and it requires only a little practice to learn to use them gracefully. The Girl on Crutches, with her ankle or toes neatly bandaged, will assuredly 1) Attract attention, and 2) Make friends easily. As to 3, the crutches will not put her in a flattering light. But they *will* win universal sympathy. What sort of man will not offer to fetch and carry for her, help her up the stairs and down the stairs, bring her a chair, a drink, a schedule, a program, make sure of her comfort, shield her injured part from careless passersby?

A dikdook of much less potency is the Arm Sling, but it

is so simple it lends itself to everyday usage, and need not be saved exclusively for vacation time. The Arm Sling can be exploited in several ways. It provides a legitimate excuse to ask someone for help with this or that, it offers a ready topic of conversation, easing those awkward first few minutes, and it serves to identify you unmistakably. You are the Girl with Her Arm in a Sling, not just a girl with brown hair and blue eyes, to be confused with ten other girls who have brown hair and blue eyes.

Speaking of hair, this too can serve as a dikdook. Of course it is necessary to have extraordinary hair if one is to rely on it for special attention. Due to the popularity of tinting and dyeing, beautiful colors are all too common. Practically the only colors left which would arouse comment, are green and peach. More effective than color is length. If you can induce your hair to grow very long so that it reaches to your hips or beyond, and if you have the courage to wear it hanging freely, you will own a natural dikdook of great value. Every man will turn to stare. You are at once seen and labeled—The Girl With Hair Down to There. You will be criticized or admired for your audacity. In either case, all men will be moved by an uncontrollable urge to pull, caress, or tangle themselves in your tresses. Conversational openings will spring to their lips easily and you will have ample opportunity to explain that you lost your hairpins, or this is the latest style from Rome, or that your doctor advised you to give your head a rest while on holiday.

It is possible an odd man here and there will shun you as a person guilty of bad taste. Each girl must for herself determine where to draw the wavering line between decorum and indecorum.

This issue must always be resolved before employing a

personal type of dikdook. Almost invariably that which is vividly arresting is also a little *outré*. If you wear a hat with a brim 28 inches wide, if your shoulder is tattooed with the American flag, if you go barefoot to a formal ball, if you wear a mask to lunch, there are bound to be raised eyebrows.

I, myself, consider the tattoo a bit vulgar. However, there is no denying that some men are fascinated by a Girl With a Tattoo. I cannot say why. For the perverse young lady who insists on this kind of decoration, there is an alternative—the decalcomania. This produces the same effect at less expense, and makes it possible to wear a different imprint to suit each occasion.

The Immense Hat is an intriguing dikdook. Men will follow it about curiously, trying to get a peek under its brim, and are never reticent about speaking to the wearer, for no man is afraid he cannot hold his own with a girl who is silly enough to wear such a big hat.

Any article of clothing that is ridiculous (and at least one such is forthcoming from the couturiers every season) makes a man agreeably conscious of his masculine superiority. If it provokes jeers, sneers, taunts, or condescending smiles, do not be dismayed. All are evidence of interest.

The Camera is a dikdook that promotes small talk. One can always turn to a man in feminine helplessness and ask for advice about openings, exposures, etc., etc. After a little conversation he is unlikely to forbid you to take his picture. And after you have taken his picture, he is unlikely to refuse to give you his address so that you can mail him a print. With a good supply of film, a girl should be able to collect a lengthy list of names and addresses together with identifying pictures. (Some say that sending photographs to the wrong names is almost certain to start a correspondence.)

In the matter of dikdooks, a girl is limited only by her inventiveness and daring. You may have read about my cousin Jennifer, who used a firework as a dikdook, with spectacular results. It was Jennifer who, while touring in Paris a few years ago, exploded a fizgig in the midst of a chamber music concert. A number of men in the audience sought her out later. Some, interpreting her action as a protest against the sluggish tempo of the scherzo, commended her warmly. Others, imagining the outburst had political significance, reprimanded her for creating a disturbance before the number had ended. Members of both groups remained to chat, and by the time the intermission was over, she had been booked for five future concerts.

I have seen kites, geiger counters, flat tires, and even revolving doors employed most successfully as conversation starters. But one should not grow dependent upon props, for these are not always available. Highly workable dikdooks may be created out of mere words. "Help! Help!" for example will bring instant attention from able-bodied males. And a man who has rescued a maid from, let us say, drowning, will not simply drop her on the beach and walk away. There is sure to be some chitchat.

Less dramatic is "Pardon me, are you Stanley Harris? My brother asked me to find you and say he can't be here." If the stranger you address thus happens to be Stanley Harris—well and good. You can have a hearty laugh over the coincidence, and shared laughter promotes amity. If (and this is more often the case) he is someone else, ask him wistfully if he will help you look for the nonexistent Mr. Harris. Hardly anything appeals to a man more than the chance to help a helpless female.

A rather nice Opening, which plays on this same masculine propensity for knight-errantry, is to approach the man with a map in hand, and some obscure spot in mind, and enlist his aid. No man can ignore the challenge of an intricately printed piece of paper, and whether or not he comprehends it, he will gladly explain it to you. The more befuddled you become, the more responsible will he feel, and like as not he will escort you to your destination. Or persuade you to change your plans and go where he is going.

One can pay a lovely compliment and provide subject matter for talk, both in one parcel, with a guileless, "Pardon me, but aren't you Tony Curtis?" If there is no other point of resemblance than that his eyes are blue, it is enough. If he is tall, mistake him for Charlton Heston. If he is fat, Peter Ustinov. And so on.

Although it is considered bad manners to stare, I hold that it is permissible when done deliberately and for a purpose. Fasten your eyes upon a likely man, and stare at him as long as he is within range. Stare stare stare. Curiosity will impel the subject to come to you and ask for an explanation. There are a number of good ones, some of which are guaranteed to have you holding hands with him within seconds:

A. "I have the strangest feeling I know you—know you intimately. We must have met in a previous incarnation." If he has anything of the mystic or the simpleton in him, he will be "hooked," as they say.

B. "You remind me of someone I once loved very deeply. A wonderful man who died [or went away or belonged to someone else]. Your brow, your smile . . . you are so much like him, I. . . ." Pause here for a little sob or a single tear. "You'll think I'm very silly but . . . would you mind holding my hand for just a minute? Till this funny feeling goes away?"

C. "There's something about your face that makes me

want to read your palm." He will promptly give you his hand and you can invent anything you like, as palmistry is not an exact science.

D. To bring yourself to the attention of someone who is not entirely unknown to you, you may employ the Dream Opening: "I dreamed about you last night." You will of course have an interesting dream ready to relate, full of Freudian symbols that indicate you are smitten with him.

Wherever practicable the Scheherazade technique may be applied. In the middle of telling a dream, or reading a palm, or giving an explanation, interrupt yourself and find an excuse to hurry away, promising to tell more when next you meet. I warrant he will hasten that next meeting, for every man is fascinated by a conversation that centers on himself.

It is not necessary to be bold in order to execute one of these Openings. They acquire a certain piquancy in the mouths of girls who are shy, timid, unsure, frightened. And that girl who, by nature or complexion, is given to blushing, possesses a rare gift—one she can use in conjunction with almost any dikdook, or by itself, as a dikdook in its own right. (I call to mind the renowned striptease artist, Blush Rosee, who aroused the interest of every man because she blushed demurely from tip to toe as she peeled.)

The value of the dikdook cannot be overestimated. For the dikdook is the link between Locating and Trapping. It is the trigger that sets everything into motion. It is the grappling iron that snatches up a total stranger and places him at your side. It is, as we say in mathematical circles, the locus of the focus.

SEVEN

Camouflage

Camouflage: *The disguising of a camp, battery, arsenal, ship, etc., as by paint, screens, shrubbery, or the like, to reduce its visibility or conceal its actual nature from the enemy. Hence, any disguise, behavior, or expedient adopted to deceive or hide.*

—MERRIAM-WEBSTER

IT IS a great mistake to deprive yourself of a dikdook in the belief that it is not for you. How often we hear the lament, "Oh, I'm too tall for anything like that." Or "too old." Or "too plain." Dear girls! dikdooks were not created for the exclusive use of standard size young beauties. They are for Every Girl.

This is not to say you should bury your head in the sand and refuse to look your cross in the eye. Imperfections do exist. They raise difficulties. They must be coped with. And I always say the best way to cope with an imperfection is to camouflage it.

Since space does not permit an extensive study of the sub-

ject, I shall touch on it lightly—*en passant*, as it were—and
trust that this little chapter may serve as a guide for each
reader in handling her own specific problem.

Let us take those items about which girls most often
complain—their height, their age, and their faces—and
attack them one by one.

The tall girl

If you are over six feet tall, I beg you, never slump,
slouch, or crouch. Nothing will emphasize your height more
than poor posture. STAND STRAIGHT!

But do not stand at all unless it is absolutely necessary.
So long as you are not vertical you are not tall. Avoid walking and dancing and golfing and marching in parades, avoid
anything that requires you to stand on your feet in juxta-
position to others who are standing on theirs.

The Beach is ideal for your purposes. There is no way of
measuring a girl who is swimming. And out of water, when

you are lounging about, half buried under sand, beach robes, beach bags, & beach umbrellas, there again your length is an unknown quantity. If the tide comes in and you must move, it is perfectly natural to crawl instead of walk, especially if you are collecting seashells.

However, you cannot make the beach a way of life, particularly if you do not dwell near the water. We must establish general rules of conduct which have a broad application. I suggest that wherever you may be, you concentrate on sitting * and sitting activities. Your height will not be noticeable while you are astride a bicycle or a horse, or while you are dining, spooning, riding in a car or train, or any other kind of vehicle (except a chariot), swiveling at a bar, playing cards or spin-the-bottle—oh, there is no end to the number of things one can do in a sitting position.

For those occasions when you have no choice but to get up off your seat, develop a repertoire of little tricks. List sharply as your escort helps you into your coat; bend down and pick lint off the carpet; run along in front of him; drop behind him; point out some object in the sky or across the street; be conscious of the slant of every pavement, and maneuver him to the high side; if you are forced to dance, dance with bended knees, and keep your head down on his shoulder. Postpone, circumvent, prevent forever if possible, the dread Moment of Truth when he must look upward to meet your eyes.

If you plot your moves, if you manage to be down when he is up and up when he is down, you may be able to win a man's affections before he notices how tall you really are. And by that time it is to be hoped he will not care.

Aside from eschewing the vertical, you should not limit

 Cultivate the ability to sit short.

or punish yourself because of your height. Disregard those narrow-minded experts who say that because you are tall you must dress quietly and behave in an inconspicuous manner. Instead of ruling out brilliant colors or whimsical styles or spectacular dikdooks—

Look to your surroundings!

Size is relative, and you can appear positively teensy silhouetted against the sky, or adrift on the ocean, or picnicking under the redwoods, or looking up from the floor of the Grand Canyon. Refuse to enter a small room or restaurant, never associate with small dogs or small people, run from low ceilings, by-pass tiny chairs, tiny cars, tiny dance floors.

☞ Keep yourself in scale

Do not lie immoderately about your height. Better to have a man say, "Isn't she a small six-footer?" than, "I never saw such a long 5′10″ in my life."

Actually, many men prefer tall girls, and strange to say this is most often true of short men. Since some of the best men are short, it is foolish to insist on a man your own size. Rarely is there a difference of more than 6 inches, and if you will measure off 6 inches on a piece of paper and look at it critically you will see that it is quite insignificant— really not enough to keep a woman and a good man apart. The more common difference of 2, 3, or 4 inches is, if viewed in the right perspective, too picayune to discuss— especially when you consider how much of married life is spent off your feet.

Small girls, too, might profit by studying this section. My Cousin Anita who is 5 feet 3 inches caught a man who is 5 feet 1 inch and she did it by following the above Rules for Tall Girls. As M. K. Stratford once said:

> *It matters not how small you be,*
> *You are too tall if you are taller than me.*

The old girl

Do not accept the fact of your age. Do not acknowledge it. Do not reveal it by word or act. Talk and laugh and dress and dance and flirt and daydream and strive according to your inclination and let the devil take all birth certificates.

You may not fool women, certainly not those who are as old as you, but men will be completely confused. For they are engagingly stupid about judging age. They assume that a woman whose dress, nails, lips, and hair are bright red, who hums all the popular tunes, and who dances the latest steps, must be young.

Because the male is so susceptible to externals it is a good idea to follow the current vogue, whatever the cost. Our flighty lords are ever drawn toward the latest model, imagining she will be better somehow than last year's model. Even men who have lived through several fashion cycles still cling to the illusion that underneath a different kind of wrapping they will find a different kind of girl. A new kind. One from the latest crop. It never occurs to them that some of these new girls are just old ones refurbished and made over.

And so, when all the young girls wear pointed witches' shoes that crush their toes, and puff up their hair till their heads are bigger than their bodies, and blacken their eyes like odalisques—go and do likewise. If you look like one of the "new girls" what does it matter how silly the new girls look!

The value of clothing and cosmetics and personal charm has been well publicized and needs no delineation here. But there is one magic accessory which has been sadly neglected. I speak of: LIGHTING.

Never take lighting for granted. Learn to find the most flattering patch of light wherever you are, to tilt your head at an angle that will compensate for overhead bulbs, and to hide from the deadly refractions that put shadows, bags, and sags on your face. A greenish bulb, a badly located chandelier, garish fluorescent fixtures can do untold harm. But a light that is the right color and the right number of watts, and shines on you from the right direction—that light carries in its fragile filament the precious gift of youth.

There is more good sense than good meter in the old limerick:

> A clever old girl from Kent
> Carried a lamp wherever she went,
> A little pink light
> That lit her just right
> And made her look young to her gent.

The plain girl

We all know that a feeling of inferiority withers the spirit and plays havoc with the gastric juices. If you are unalterably, uncompromisingly plain, pray do not give yourself the added burden of a harmful complex, when in truth you have every reason to be full of confidence and cheer. I do not say this with the obtusity of a Pollyanna, but with the authority of an authority who has researched her subject thoroughly. You may find proof for yourself by making this simple experiment:

> Go forth early one morning and ring the doorbells of a thousand homes. Look at the faces of the housewives who come to the door. You will be persuaded beyond doubt that plain girls can and do win husbands.

As a matter of record, the plain girl is the type of girl almost every man takes for a wife. He may not *want* to take her. He may prefer a beautiful wife. But the supply of beauties is extremely limited and most men must perforce take run-of-the-mill.

An amusing facet of this situation is that nine times out of ten the man does not suspect that what he is getting is not a beauty. It is said, with some bitterness, that man is superficial, that he is to be won only by a pretty face and figure. La! He is more superficial than that. It is not even the face and figure, but the *decorations* on the face and figure that intrigue his fancy and ravish his heart.

Moreover, so lacking is he in taste and discernment that he does not know pretty from flashy, svelte from skinny, curvaceous from chubby, feminine from slutty. I have a sister whose beauty made her overconfident, and on a dare she went to a masquerade party sans jewelry and cosmetics, and clad in a potato sack. She spent a wretched evening, but learned a lesson, one that we all might heed: "Beauty bare" is not enough.

The eye of man is primitive and must be captured by primitive means. He is entranced by anything that glitters, shimmies, twinkles, or tinkles. My father's broker was caught by a single sequin, winking in the navel of a very plain girl.

Avail yourself of every ... (If you are wondering how he happened to see it, she was lying on the beach in a bikini under a huge pink umbrella. Incidentally, this girl was 6 feet tall and forty-five years of age.) Avail yourself of every aid and dikdook known to woman. Bedeck your person with bells and bows and bangles and beauty patches, and sprinkle stardust in your hair. The plainer you are, the more need you have of all the frou-frou and la-di-da you can muster.

Whatever your imperfection, make liberal use of camouflage. The most famous beauties of our day are put together by artisans. The hairdresser supplies their hair, the dentist caps their teeth, the surgeon erases their wrinkles, the corsetiere sews perfectly molded torsos into their clothes. We do not admire these lovely creatures the less for it. We are inclined to applaud the sow's ear that turns itself into a silk purse.

Think of yourself as a doll fresh from the factory, and do whatever is necessary to make yourself the most fetching doll possible, thanking your stars that you live in an age when science is the handmaid of womankind.

———•◆•———

EIGHT

How to Trap Him

I will find a way or make one.

—HANNIBAL

THERE IS no one Perfect Plan which can be used against all men. This is because each man has his own peculiar tastes, and sometimes these are very peculiar indeed. One man adores the naive childlike female, another is charmed by the gruff domineering lady-sergeant. Some cannot resist the solid virtues, others prefer the exotic or the quixotic. The very attributes that intrigue John will leave Bert indifferent, intimidate Claude, and antagonize Morris.

It is said that there is a lid for every pot—a homely adage, which suggests that each one gets what she deserves and that this is a fair dispensation. I cannot subscribe to such a theory. Firstly, the Fates operate in such a slipshod fashion that even if the correct lid for a specific girl does exist somewhere, it is quite likely she will never come across it. Secondly, there are some who do not want a matching lid; they aspire to something better.

A realistic girl goes after whatever is available. She will bend, twist, stretch, or shrink, to fit the lid she is trying to acquire. Once she has it firmly secured she can resume her natural form and set about altering the lid so that *it* will conform to *her*. (It is interesting to observe the struggle that goes on in most marriages, each partner trying to hammer the other into the desired shape.)

Here a question of ethics forces itself upon us: Is it fair to pretend to be what you are not? Allow me to point out that esteemed members of Congress are different men after election than before, that widely advertised products do not live up to their promises, and that great nations deal falsely with one another.

Is it fair, in a civilization which teeters on a foundation of treachery, trickery, and trumpery, to demand that the Single Girl bear the onus of honesty? I think not!

Therefore, it is without apology that I describe here, in detail, the Lures, Spellbinders, Traps, Formulas, and Love Potions used in capturing a husband. Some are complicated, some are simple. A few may seem too transparent. Do not dismiss these as worthless. That which to us is obvious and hackneyed enough to be laughable, is apt to be accepted by the male without question. Though they are full of guile when stalking the female for their own wicked purposes, they are not always able to recognize guile when it is turned against them. After they are married they look back in astonishment at the childish mistakes they made, and wonder how they could have been taken in by such ancient tricks.

In order to present a comprehensive collection of the best, time-tested Lures, Spellbinders, Traps, Formulas, and Love Potions, I find it necessary to include several which are really not quite nice. These are *not recommended*. They are merely reported. I trust each girl will know which method is right for her and—what is vastly more important —which method is right for the man on whom she is working.

———————◆———————

NINE

The Lures

Lure 1: Home and Hearth

THIS IS the grandmother of all lures, and the most respected method in the repertoire. Young girls and old girls, sophisticated and unsophisticated, all may use it. And any man who does not live with a doting female relative is vulnerable to its attractions.

The premise is sound: Give a bachelor a rich dose of the comforts he lacks and he will become soft, spoiled, unfit for the rigors of single life.

The Home and Hearth girl keeps a watchful eye on the man she is luring. Does he have all his buttons? Is there a hole in his sock? Is his jacket fraying at the elbows? She is ever ready to whip out her little sewing kit. Does he hate to shop? She will sacrifice her lunch hour to buy what he needs. She takes his shoes to the cobbler, shampoos his hair, nurses him when he is ill, walks his dog, entertains his visiting aunt, and argues with his landlord about the plumbing.

Above all, she cooks for him. Home cooking is the strongest feature of Lure 1. My Aunt Amelia caught Uncle Ted on it although she could not cook an egg. She invited him each week for a home-cooked dinner, secretly had the food brought in from a fine caterer, served it to him herself, and had the advantage of coming to the table fresh and lovely, unwearied by culinary chores.

A girl who has few domestic talents does not hesitate to hire experts, as Aunt Amelia did. A fancy laundress, a capable tailor, are invaluable aids. But in the main, the girl who uses this Lure spends a great deal of energy on the man she is cozening. It is her hope that he will think, "What a convenience she is! How handy it is to have her on hand!" and that in order to insure his continued comfort, he will ask her to marry him.

If he does not do so within a reasonable time, she cuts off her services without notice. This is like pulling a soft bed out from under a slumbering man, and the rude jolt will sometimes force a hasty proposal. Thus, victory may come after the Lure is withdrawn, which is why experts affectionately refer to this method as Janus—it has a good bite both coming and going.

Many girls complain that the Home and Hearth is too exhausting, but those who believe in it say, "Who's afraid of a little work? There'll be plenty of time to sit back and take things easy after I'm married."

Lure 2: Fair Damsel to the Rescue

It is not uncommon to come upon a desirable man who is locked fast in his mother's grip. Bewitched by this Dragon-mother he cannot be pried loose by outside force, nor can he be induced to free himself, and so hopeless does the situation seem that the average girl will shake her head sadly and give up the Captive Prince without a struggle.

This is too bad, for the Dragon-mother can be vanquished. If her hands are kissed and licked they gradually loosen their grip, if she is flattered and wooed she becomes friendly instead of forbidding, if she is convinced that she will acquire a faithful slave instead of a rival she will in the end accept a daughter-in-law.

I have seen Lure 2 in operation, and the Fair Damsel does not have much fun in the courtship period. She dances continual attendance on this Dragon she longs to call "mother-in-law." She rings It often on the telephone when the Prince is at work, and she comes to visit, and does all manner of things to endear herself to It. She manicures Its claws and home-permanents Its tresses and helps It with the marketing and cooking. She brings It candy and flowers, and pretty trifles for Its mantlepiece. She invites It out on twosomes, taking It to a church luncheon or the races or wherever It would like to go.

And when the Prince is on hand this valiant maid insists that every date include the Dragon, and be centered on the Dragon's pleasure, and that the Dragon sit between them, and that the Dragon have the first dance. Should a difference of opinion occur between Dragon and Son, the Damsel always sides with the Dragon. And to any who will listen she speaks of the monster with glowing admiration.

When at last marriage is discussed, she placates the Dragon with assurances that It will be queen of the household. Right up to the wedding day she defers to It in all things, even unto the length of the bridal veil.

I recently attended a wedding where the groom's mother changed into traveling clothes after the reception. I questioned the bride about this as she changed her own costume.

"Yes," she giggled, "his dear Mother planned right from the beginning to come along to Mexico for the honeymoon. However, I persuaded her it would be undignified to ride off with us in a shower of rice and old shoes, so we are driving to the railroad station in separate limousines." She removed her veil and tossed it gaily onto the chandelier.

"Now, although Kenneth doesn't know it, his dear Mother and her luggage are going to be put on the Broadway Ltd., headed for New York. My bridegroom and I will be well on our way toward the Rio Grande by the time she realizes we are not on the same train." She smiled mischievously. "I can just picture the Old Dragon ransacking every compartment looking for her lost boy, while I comfort him with hugs and kisses and assure him Mother dear must have wanted it this way."

That girl had pluck! Not often does a bride have the courage to fool her husband and start mistreating her mother-in-law so promptly after the wedding. But the courage, the determination, and the usurping of the Dragon's position—these are part of a familiar and time-hallowed tradition.

There is a lesson for everyone in Lure 2: It is not necessary that you like a man's mother, only that you make her like you. This is recommended even when she is not a Dragon. Once the marriage is consummated a girl can safely slight her mother-in-law in the traditional manner. There are few cases on record where an indignant mother was able to take back her son.

Lure 3: Miss Patience

This Lure has but one ingredient—patience. Miss Patience will wait and work, month after month, on a desired man, though she fully realizes she is not his match. Undaunted by his superiority and his indifference, she is available whenever he has time for her.

Miss Patience is not as humble as she appears. Because Lure 3 requires little time and energy, she manages it with her left hand, while with her right hand she is busily engaged in pursuing a different man with a different method (or vice versa if she is left-handed, as so many of us are since educators decided it is dangerous to tamper with some —though fortunately not *all*—of our natural tendencies).

This ambidextrous lass is always ready to break a date or change her plans to accommodate the man on whom she is practicing her patience. If his best friend unexpectedly deserts him, she will fill in the empty evening. If his TV set breaks down, he is welcome to share hers. If he has spent too much money entertaining other girls, he can even things up by letting Miss Patience take him to the movies. She will gladly give him dinner on these occasions. And if she can get rid of her parents or roommate, there will be a pleasant interlude of petting.

All this is granted on short notice. The patient girl never reproaches him for phoning at the last moment, never balks at going out with him in a snowstorm, even when he tactlessly informs her that the girl he originally invited fell sick. Unsuspectingly he begins to rely on this relationship, which is so convenient and inexpensive, and flattering to his ego. His guard is down. What is there to fear, he thinks, from an undemanding girl who understands full well he is too good for her?

When a male relaxes with a female, trusting and unafraid, he is a Samson sleeping in a barber's chair. Unless angels are watching over him, he is sure to be clipped.

If the angels are on *her* side the climax comes, inexplicably, one quiet evening while he is in her arms. A sudden surge of gratitude or affection, or an impulse from a cosmic source, or a spiteful need to punish some better girl who has mistreated him, and he finds his surprised lips proposing marriage.

Of course, this does not always happen. Often as not, Miss Patience's patience goes unrewarded. But, for a method that can be worked on the side, in one's spare time, and has a superior man as the prize, Lure 3 must be rated as exceedingly worthwhile.

Lure 4: Sick Sick Sick

I have heard it said that marriage to a hypochondriac is unbearable. What an absurd idea! The hypochondriac makes no worse a husband than any other man. We marry gamblers, philanderers, boors, bores, boozers, bullies, loafers, braggarts, misers, spendthrifts, hypocrites, misogynists, and clowns. Why draw the line at hypochondriacs?

The girl who is working on a hypochondriac pretends to be as preoccupied with his ailments as he is. She does, in fact, become thoroughly familiar with them, so that she can

discuss them with him at length. She saves clippings that refer to his specialty, reports anything she has heard, investigates new theories or cures. She spends long evenings with him, examining his X-rays and counting and assorting his pills. Never does she switch the conversation away from his favorite topic, or belittle the importance of his affliction, or compare it with one that is more serious. And never never does she allow such words as "psychosomatic" or "psychological" or "hypochondriacal" to pass her lips.

The imaginary invalid, accustomed to the jeers of friends, relatives, and doctors, thinks he has found Heaven when he meets a woman who liberally dispenses sympathy and remedies. Without pausing to examine her virtues or her vices, he gallops cheerfully to the altar—willing, nay, *eager* to make her his lawful wedded nurse.

Marriage often cures a man of hypochondria. However, this cannot be attributed to the salutary effect of being coddled by a loving wife. On the contrary. The girl who catches her husband with Lure 4 apparently exhausts her fund of sympathy and patience during courtship, for before the honeymoon is over, she proceeds to knock his hypochondria out of him (so to speak) by means of ridicule, threats, indifference, scolding, or enforced psychiatric treatment.

Lure 5: Big Name Hunter

Every famous or near-famous man is highly susceptible to a girl who worships at his feet. When he is unattractive or uncouth (and so many of them are) he is pathetically grateful for the delicious feminine attentions which were denied him in his days of obscurity. Attractive men, accustomed to adulation, are dependent on it, and when they become famous the need is magnified. Whether ugly as

September 15, 7

ある日に Liza のお誕生日を祝う為に Sequoia Park、

ドライブで一時間位へ、

Behan or handsome as Burton, the important, great, or famous man is constantly hungry for assurance that he is important, great, or famous.

Unless she can get near him through her work or social contacts, the girl whose heart is set on acquiring a Big Name has one hurdle to clear—getting to meet him. A short note on good stationery, expressing sincere admiration, is one way of accomplishing this. Only cinema stars are surfeited with these paper bouquets, and far too few are received by other famous persons.

The great athletes, surgeons, statesmen, artists, scholars, tycoons, religious leaders, authors, lawyers, scientists—how they yearn for a little written tribute. How disappointed they are each morning when the postman brings only bills, dividends, advertisements, and requests for charity. And how touched they are, how elated, how excited, how thankful, when a little homage arrives in an envelope.

To this evidence of his famousness, this proof of his popularity, the Big Name is very likely to respond—unless he is lazy or busy, or overprotected by a watchful secretary. Sometimes, before a reply can be coaxed from him, it is necessary to send several letters, filled with compliments and earnest questions related to his calling. But once a correspondence is established it is not too difficult to effect a meeting.

There are, to be sure, more direct, more speedy ways for a young lady to worm herself into a seemingly unapproachable stronghold.* She may simply ring the great man's doorbell and ask to speak with him. (Often enough he will open the door himself in his shirt sleeves.) Or she may waylay

 A classic example is the case of the great Barrymore, who was besieged on his sickbed by a worshipful young admirer, and carried straight from the hospital to the altar.

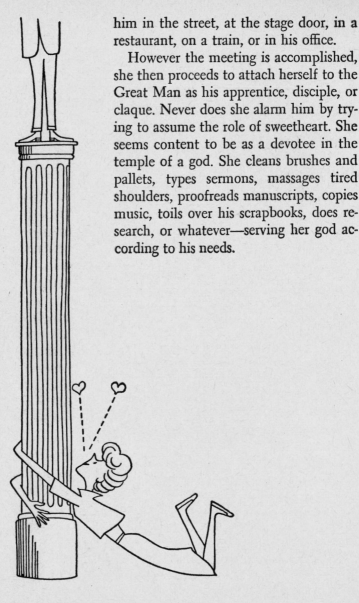

him in the street, at the stage door, in a restaurant, on a train, or in his office.

However the meeting is accomplished, she then proceeds to attach herself to the Great Man as his apprentice, disciple, or claque. Never does she alarm him by trying to assume the role of sweetheart. She seems content to be as a devotee in the temple of a god. She cleans brushes and pallets, types sermons, massages tired shoulders, proofreads manuscripts, copies music, toils over his scrapbooks, does research, or whatever—serving her god according to his needs.

"Let me do it for you, Sir," or "Maestro," she begs. "If I can serve the great So-and-So I will feel I have a function in society."

Ceaselessly she performs her function. She blows up to giant-size his every little triumph, scourges his critics and rivals, and reminds him regularly that the world reveres him. What human male, famous or near famous, will not want to hold on to a female who sits at his feet and calls up to him again and again that he is great Great GREAT! Here is the synthesis, the symbol of the public acclaim he craves.

Anyone who has fought his way to fame is accustomed to the horrid flavor of disappointment, and is therefore able to swallow it without choking when he discovers after the wedding that the creature he has clasped to his breast can be as demanding, indifferent, unpredictable, and harsh as the public she symbolizes.

As to the one who came upon fame easily, and has not learned how to swallow anything that is not sweet—he, alas, may choke.

Lure 6: Green Apples

When ripe apples are scarce or out of reach the wise man will content himself with a green one. —ANON.

Since pickers in general deem green apples beneath consideration, the supply is always ample and the pickings are easy. Arbitrarily equating men with apples, the perpetrator of this Lure reaches out for a youth of eighteen or nineteen. She herself is often young, a girl in her mid-twenties, alarmed by a lack of prospects and unnerved by the weddings of her friends. Or she may be older, and arrived at a point of ruthless determination. In either case she dips into the age bracket where there is a superabundance of single males and selects one for herself. (He may be a little older than nineteen, provided he is still green. And, too, he may be younger than eighteen, if she has the patience to cultivate him until he is full grown.)

Success with this Lure is almost guaranteed. The mere fact that an older woman looks upon him as a MAN is enough to addle a boy's brains. Moreover, he is convinced that all the vague but urgent yearnings to prove his manhood will find expression under her guidance. How childish his contemporaries seem, crashing awkwardly through taboos with inexperienced little girls, wondering how to win the respect of headwaiters and ushers, performing reckless, lawless acts of adolescent defiance, striving to make people realize they are no longer to be regarded as children. He smiles condescendingly upon these former playmates as he leaps into instant adulthood on the arm of his adult woman.

When marriage is proposed he is undaunted, and plunges into it with the same cocky air worn by young soldiers rushing onto the battlefield. Youth and Ignorance know no fear, it is said (and sometimes it is true).

In those instances where a Green Apple has sufficient intelligence to be frightened by Marriage and to hesitate, he can be easily nudged into making the step. Here is a typical scene in which a smart apple is cooked according to Lure 6:

SHE (Kissing him tenderly) Timmy darling, I am afraid we must stop seeing each other.

HE (Blanching) Stop? But why?

SHE You are too young for me.

HE (He gasps) Too young? Too young! Me? You said I was more mature than other men twice my age!

SHE Except for one thing. You're too young for that.

98

HE Too young for what?

SHE Marriage.

HE (Struck dumb by this dazzling new idea) Marriage?

SHE Yes. *You* know. . . . Marriage.

HE Oh. (He gulps nervously, and his eyes dart about the room as if looking for an escape hatch)

SHE You see, darling . . . I just don't think you're ready.

HE For . . . Marriage?

SHE Yes, marriage.

HE Well, I could . . . I could *get* ready, maybe . . . in two, three years. What do you say? Or four or five years?

SHE *I'm* ready *now*.

HE But gosh . . . everything's so great the way it is!

SHE Not for me it isn't.

(He bites his finger nails and looks stubbornly at his shoe)

SHE I'm returning your books and records and athletic trophies. There's the package, all neatly tied.

HE (Throwing himself down on the sofa with a heartrending groan) Keep it for a souvenir!

SHE No, Timmy . . . no loose ends. But you needn't hurry about returning the things I gave you—the hi-fi and the typewriter and the rifle and the motorcycle. You can bring them around next week.

HE (He sits up slowly, staring at her as if she has stabbed him in the back) Dolores! Can't we talk about it?

SHE What for! I'm sure your parents won't allow you to get married.

HE (This is the last straw) Do you think I'm a child or something? My parents can't tell me what to do. If I want to get married, I'll get married!

SHE Oh Timmy, I do admire your independent spirit!

I will end the scene at this point, for you can well imagine all that he said and all that she said and how it all turned out.

The girl who takes a very young husband must be prepared to support him while he finishes school, or until he begins to earn an adequate income for two. But the sacrifice is worthwhile. In return she will have a perfectly good man, trained to her liking, and capable of giving extra years of service at the other end of their marriage.

Lure 7: Fountain of Youth

Success favors the girl who dares to venture out of her age bracket in either direction, though it must be noted that opportunities are fewer among the elderly. Males have a tendency to die off at a more rapid rate than females, a lamentable weakness which medical science is striving to remedy. But the ones who survive are, in their declining years, excellent material for matrimony.

A girl who decides to try for one of these will not have to wonder if he is going to lose his hair, or his teeth, or his vitality. Nor need she weigh the imponderables of success and fortune—his condition is already established. He is no pig-in-a-poke—she knows what she is getting.

Above all, she knows she will have peace of mind. The average wife lives in fear that despite the mortality tables she may die before her husband, and he will squander their hard-gotten savings on a second wife. But the young wife of an old husband almost invariably *is* that lucky second wife, and has little doubt that she will be the last.

Though she be devoid of beauty and money and charm, a young or youngish girl may still succeed in luring an oldish man into marrying her. She cannot make capital of her

Youth in courting a *young* man. Because he himself has it, he takes the precious asset for granted. But to an older man, who has had it and lost it, who looks enviously at those who still have it, and hopes somehow to recapture it or taste of it again—to him, any female who has it is a shining symbol of all that he desires.

She who practices Lure 7 plays on this vulnerability. She refuses to let her old boy say he is old, she insists age is measured by the spirit and not by the calendar, she discovers all sorts of young traits in him, and encourages him to indulge in juvenile follies. While pretending he is inexhaustible she avoids any activity that will tire him. She allows him to outstrip her in walking, dancing, and the like, leans on him (lightly) to prove his superior strength, and vows she has never met a young man who was his equal. Rejuvenated, revitalized, he does not have to be coaxed into making this Fountain of Youth his exclusive property, but hobbles spryly to the altar.

This kind of match incurs a certain amount of public disapproval, for a girl marries an old man only when he is wealthy or famous or both, and this gives rise to the suspicion that her motive is materialistic. Even the old man himself is sometimes inclined to be skeptical.

But, attributing all criticism to envy or cynicism, the girl who uses Lure 7 refuses to be embarrassed. She insists she is merely making an honest effort to secure a wedding ring, and she asks her critics (with some justification, it must be admitted) "What sort of person would I be to marry a *poor* old man, and burden him in the winter of his life with the upkeep of a new young wife?"

TEN

The Traps

Trap 1: The Confidence Game

ONLY AN unscrupulous or a desperate girl will resort to this Trap. And she must, moreover, have an unscrupulous or desperate parent.*

I need hardly describe here how The Confidence Game is played, since everyone has read of it, seen it in the theater, or known some unfortunate male who was caught by means of it. Briefly, it is Compromise by Prearrangement. A relative "surprises" the Confidence Girl and her victim in a critical situation, makes an angry scene, and insists that only Marriage will satisfy the family honor.

 An unscrupulous brother or some other responsible relative will also do.

A man so trapped is in no position to argue, especially if he works for the girl's father, is the son of friends or neighbors, comes from a good family, is easily intimidated, or holds a position that cannot bear a scandal—such as teacher, pastor, doctor, Scout master, or the like. A girl wily enough to use the #1 Trap will not make the mistake of wasting her efforts on a local ne'er-do-well, or a traveling salesman, or an actor (who would only benefit by bad publicity).

When Trap 1 fails, it is usually because the third party, the relative, is not conscientious and reliable. I call to mind the case of a Nashville girl who dearly loved a young man

who dated her occasionally. She invited him into the living room late one night, intimating the family was away, although she had hidden her father in the kitchen. The father was to make a dramatic entrance at 12:30 and discover his daughter with her blouse unfastened—evidence enough to outrage any parent. But the appointed moment came and went without interruption and the minutes ticked away. By 12:45 her blouse was under the sofa and still no father came to the rescue. By one o'clock this naughty girl, hoisted with her own petard, had forfeited her dearest possession. All because her father had become engrossed in a Perry Mason mystery and lost track of the time.

(I must mention, in passing, that the betrayed daughter, being a person of strong will, turned her loss into a victory by utilizing another scandalous Trap, Number 2.)

It occasionally happens that an innocent girl is truly surprised while overstepping the limits of propriety. One can only sympathize with her and hope that the intruding relative is firm enough and menacing enough to frighten the guilty man into marriage.

There is no way to distinguish between the arranged and the unarranged scene, for the guileful girl will weep as loud and pitifully as the guileless one, and even the most sophisticated victim will wonder, long after the wedding bells have tolled his knell, whether he was duped or just unlucky.

Trap 2: The Great Deception

This Trap is the most reprehensible of all the Methods. Women blush for their sex when it is mentioned, and men caught in its pitiless jaws cry Foul! I speak of—and I wish I did not have to speak of it—the false claim of approaching motherhood.

Statistics show that last year

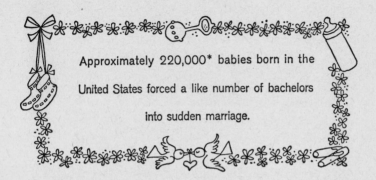

Approximately 220,000* babies born in the United States forced a like number of bachelors into sudden marriage.

These are the figures for a typical year. It is heartening to know that so many bachelors, on being confronted with impending parenthood, marry the offended girl. Such behavior speaks well for the American male's sense of responsibility and fair play. But, sad to say, this high-minded decency makes him easy prey for the unscrupulous type of girl who *pretends* he has put her on the road to motherhood.

Though there are no authenticated figures available, it is well known that countless males marry because of a misconception. For every real unborn baby who precipitates a wedding, I daresay there are two hypothetical ones who do the same. Shocking, is it not?

 According to Harold T. Christensen's "conservative estimate" in the Official Journal of the American Sociological Society: One out of every five legitimate first-born babies is conceived out of wedlock.
   This means that every time you see five proud mothers displaying their firstborn you can be reasonably sure that one of those mothers had a near squeak.

I recently took the opportunity to question a girl who had used Trap 2 to bully a fine young man into marrying her. "How do you justify yourself?" I asked politely.

"Your Cousin Randolph," she replied, "used every trick in the book * to seduce me. Was I not justified in using whatever means I could, to make him marry me? Tit for tat, you know."

I forgave her with all my heart. It is difficult to be angry with a girl who, having inadvertently surrendered herself to a persuasive man, seeks to remedy the error by means of The Great Deception.

But to the calculating Miss who is deliberately planning to misbehave in order to qualify herself for Trap 2, I say, Shame. I also say, My dear dear girl, think it over! "The best laid schemes o' maids and men gang aft agley." You may, heaven forbid, come a cropper and when you discover your make-believe is not a make-believe at all, you will have these tragic (and *authentic*) figures to contemplate: One out of 5¼ babies conceived outside of wedlock is destined to be illegitimate!

This proof that one out of 5¼ bachelor fathers has no sense of fair play should give pause to every girl.

> "No one can build his security upon the nobleness of another person."   —WILLA CATHER

Trap 3: Come into My Parlor

Wanted: Bachelor, young, steadily employed, to rent beautiful bed-sitting room in private residence. References required.

 I presume she was referring to my book *The Unfair Sex.*

An advertisement similar to the one above is the opening action in Trap 3. "Middle-aged" or "elderly" may be substituted for "young," "widower" for "bachelor," "professional man" for "steadily employed," and other requirements added, all according to the tastes of the landlady who is advertising. No other Method allows so much freedom in specifying exactly what is desired in a husband.

The female who has a room to rent occupies a commanding position. In the comfort of her own parlor she may sit back and interview a stream of qualified men. It is her privilege to ask each one impertinent questions about his personal habits, likes and dislikes, and financial status.

Fully informed, she may evaluate the candidates, select the one she likes best, and then with the utmost propriety invite him to live in her home—for a fixed fee.

What a priceless advantage it is to have the chosen one in a position where he can be steadily under attack. The landlady can so easily win the gratitude, affection, and finally the dependence of the lone male under her roof. She serves him delectable breakfasts, brings him the Sunday newspapers, takes over the care of his laundry, invites him to dinner occasionally. She does not complain about his untidiness or the blaring of his radio. Only smiles and sweet words and thoughtful acts are showered upon him, and never does she show herself with curlers in her hair.

She will of course have an older (much older) female living with her as a sort of unofficial duenna. The duenna will know when to be present, when to be absent, and when to sing the landlady's praises.

There are no lonely evenings for the Boarder. He soon learns that he is welcome in the parlor for checkers or cards or TV or just for conversation. He may also enter the kitchen, the holy of holies, whenever he has a mind to, and ransack the refrigerator or the cookie jar.

He lives like a lord in this lady's castle. Only one door is closed to him—the door of the lady's bedchamber. When a human being is accorded every freedom—excepting only one—he finds that single restriction insupportable. He will go to any length, even marriage, to remove it.

However, it sometimes happens that the Boarder is not the least bit fond of his landlady, or he is a Mr. O, or he has a dear friend on the outside, or he is strongly opposed to marriage—and he will politely respect the Closed Door. Such a Boarder will be invited to move out, as his room "is needed for an uncle" or "an old friend."

Seldom does a contented Boarder accept dismissal. The natural inertia of man makes him loath to change any established situation. He finds it difficult, even when conditions are very bad, to bring things to a halt, make a decision, and strike out on a new path with its unforeseeable disadvantages. How much more difficult it is for him to leave a gracious castle—and know that some other male will move in to enjoy all that was his.

Bent on retaining his sovereignty, he quickly enters into marriage. Just as quickly he discovers he is no longer his lady's lord but her vassal. Lackaday! The drawbridge is up, and there is no escape.

Trap 4: No No No

This age-old trap is one of those most abominated by men, and in truth it is easy to see why it makes them so angry. It is designed to trap the Trapper, to fool the Fooler —it is a turning of the tables, and no one likes that, except the one who does the turning.

To put it simply, a girl pretends to be succumbing to seduction, and when her seducer has grown sanguine with the expectation of victory, she suddenly cries out, "No, no, no!" This she does on one occasion after another, protesting each time that she is afraid to see him again, but seeing him nevertheless, and stunning him anew with her No No No just when he thinks he has won.

If the victim is the kind of man who cannot bear to put aside a suspense story until he reaches the end, he will be unable to put aside this teasing lass. The No No No Girl can make a man so dizzy with frustration that he will stagger straight into the Trap, gasping "I do I do," to prevent her from saying "No no" to him again.

Trap 5: Shadow Play

Closely related to Number 4 is Number 5, which likewise utilizes the fundamental principle of Baiting, but only as an adjunct to the malicious device of Provoking Jealousy. The following little drama illustrates the Method in operation.

PLACE: Divan in her living room
TIME: Midnight

He and She have been seeing each other often. She has decided she wants him for a husband but he has never mentioned the word marriage. She knows she must not drift and has decided to shape the course of destiny.

HE (Kissing her with feeling) Happy?
SHE (Returning his kisses) Mmm.
(His kisses grow more ardent and finally she pulls away from him) Archie! Please. You mustn't.
HE Sweetheart. Don't you want me close to you?
SHE Oh I do. I do, Archie dear. But I must think of my husband.
HE Your husband!! You have no husband!!
SHE Not yet. But some day, Archie, I shall have one, and I've got to protect his honor, haven't I?
HE Oh, come! This is the twentieth century. No man expects to marry a saint. You're allowed to have a little fun.
SHE (Shocked) Archie! If you found your wife in another man's arms, would you call it a "little fun?"
HE But you're not married! You haven't even met the guy.
SHE That's not the point. He's someplace, and he's going to

be my husband and I want to behave in a way he'd approve of.

We will interrupt the Shadow Play here and pick it up again later, after some days or weeks have elapsed. Picture this couple in the meantime, repeating more or less the same words and actions recorded above. Though Archie may plead and argue and coax, nothing can shake this girl's resolve to be faithful to her future husband.

The situation, though it appears to be a stalemate, is rich in advantages to the girl: (a) Without appearing bold, she has introduced the subject of marriage and put it squarely in the forefront of their relationship; (b) She has demonstrated what a faithful wife she will be; and (c) She has set up a rival, the irritating, tormenting shadow of an unknown man.

The exasperated boyfriend has two courses of action open to him, both profitable to the girl. If he is seriously opposed to marriage he will be alarmed by her frequent allusions to a husband, and he will drop her. A girl is well rid of such a man, and the sooner the better. If, on the other hand, he is of the material from which husbands are made, he will react to the Shadow like a small boy who is presented with a baby brother. He will be infuriated when told he cannot do this because it might distress the Shadow, and he cannot have that because it is being saved for the Shadow, and the other thing is forbidden since it rightfully belongs to the Shadow. Even if he is not enamored of the girl, he will be bitterly jealous of the outsider who stands between him and what he wants. How can he brook the thought that an unknown stranger, a cypher, outranks him in importance! Each reference to the husband will drive him closer to the breaking point, until at last there arrives the hoped for denouement of the Shadow Play:

SHE Oh no, Archie dear, that's one of the things I'm saving for my husband,. Now you'll have to sit up, and take your feet off the couch, and put your shoes back on.

HE I won't.

SHE Please, Archie . . . out of respect for my husband.

HE Your husband be damned! I'm tired of hearing about your husband. I got here first, and you're marrying *me*. Now, what has he got to say to *that!*

SHE (Soothing his scowling brow) Why, I don't care what he says, darling. *You're* the only one who counts now. (Satisfied, he puts his head on her lap. He has triumphed at last over his hated rival.)

CURTAIN

Trap 6: The Helpmeet

This is effective against younger men not yet established in their careers, and older ones who are in the same position. The Helpmeet loudly declares that it is a wife's duty to support her husband until he has attained Success. And she ostentatiously flourishes a pay check that is adequate and regular, to prove that she can do it.

Artists, particularly—writers, painters, composers, actors, all those in the hopeless professions—find such an attitude most appealing. Inventors, too, and scholars and failures are eager to be subsidized.

Tempted by the promise of Security while Struggling, touched by the Helpmeet's complete confidence in his future, flattered by her honeyed phrases of praises, a man will trustingly sign the marriage certificate. It does not enter his mind that although he is making a legal contract to support the Helpmeet, all her promises to support him are merely words words words.

Sometimes the Helpmeet really helps, but all too frequently she has no intention of sticking by her bargain, and he will be obliged to abandon some fascinating profession and spend his life selling railroad tickets or insurance policies to provide for the welsher and her offspring.

Trap 7: Stolen Sweets

Chaucer wrote, "Forbid us thing, that thing desyren we." This profound observation is the inspiration for Trap 7, which relies on the fact that the girl who cannot be openly courted has a very special attraction. One who is locked in a tower, or languishes apart under the stern eye of a maiden aunt, or is held captive in a girls' finishing school—that sort of girl always inspires the sort of man who is willing to risk all to attain the unattainable.

One might think that Number 7 is a rather outmoded Method, ill-suited to the girl of today, who has complete freedom. But no. It was used successfully only last year by a dear cousin of mine, who because of her romantic nature and a talent for fibbing, found Stolen Sweets an ideal vehicle.

She never permitted her boyfriend to call for her at her home, but met them secretly, and often nervously and with misgivings. "They won't allow me to have dates," she would confide tragically. "They don't want me to get married— they're determined to keep me with them always."

Her escort was more than an escort—he was a knight-errant, a conspirator, a fellow rebel against tyranny. There was about all her dates a cloak-and-dagger atmosphere. An evening at a night club was a breathless adventure, with possible informers lurking everywhere. A day in the country was a hard-won bit of happiness, planned and plotted and boldly risked. Telephone calls were prearranged for an exact moment, and answered in whispers after half a ring.

Many were intrigued by the unique experience of having to steal their sweets. One young man, who could not tolerate parental authority, was inflamed with a desire to confront my cousin's parents and protest against their cruel and possessive attitude. On being persuaded that this would result only in harsher restrictions, the hot-blooded youth proposed mutiny. If she were to marry, he pointed out, her parents would no longer have any authority over her—she would owe obedience only to her husband (sic).

Quaking with counterfeit fear, the ingenious girl allowed herself to be persuaded to run away with him. It happened that I was there when she came home to present her bride-groom to her parents, and I shall never forget how dazed and amazed he was by the warm welcome he received from his overjoyed father- and mother-in-law.

Trap 8: The Mouse Trap

Men fear marriage for many reasons. One is a dread of being henpecked. Remembering how they were ruled by their mothers during childhood they are reluctant to give themselves over to another female boss. Many girls allay this fear by using Trap 8.

The girl who is pretending to be a Mouse expresses no opinions of her own, but echoes those of the man she is trying to trap. She has no wishes but his wishes, no likes, no dislikes, only his.

Here is a picture of a Mouse playing with a Cat.

THE PLACE: A Restaurant
THE TIME: After the theater

HE What would you like?
SHE What are you having?
HE *Truite almondine.*
SHE I'll have that too.
HE What wine?
SHE Sauterne?
HE Sauterne!?
SHE (Worried) It's white for fish, isn't it? Or is it?
HE I prefer Claret.
SHE Of course. Claret for almonds! You are so right.
HE As a matter of fact I'm wrong. . . .
SHE Oh . . .
HE . . . but I'm having Claret anyhow.

SHE Then that's what I'll have too.

HE Good. Claret . . . to match your red dress.

SHE (Shuddering as she visualizes how the two reds will clash) What a thoughtful thought.

HE (Putting aside menu) Now, where were we?

SHE We were discussing the play. You liked the actor who played Morell, but you thought the Candida looked too young.

HE Do you agree?

SHE Definitely.

HE What do you think of the play itself?

SHE Oh, there's nothing to criticize when it's Shaw. (doubtfully) Is there?

HE What about the character of Candida?

SHE (Cautiously) Candida? Why, she's . . . *everyone loves* Candida.

HE Not *I*. I can't stand her.

SHE (Stunned) Oh . . . Well, to tell the truth, neither can I!

HE Good girl. I'm glad to hear that.

SHE (After a moment) Uh . . . why don't we like her?

HE Because she's a smug, opinionated female who thinks she *knows* all and *is* all to all men.

SHE She is? I mean, she *is!* I've always thought so.

HE If ever a woman loved herself, it's Candida. What's more, she's vain and she's insincere. She leads Marchbanks on, and then priggishly puts him off.

SHE . . . puts him off. Yes.

HE She speaks to her husband as if he were a backward child, and takes away his last crumb of manly pride. She makes it quite plain that she doesn't need him but is staying with him only because she thinks he's a poor fool who could never get through a day without her to lean on.

116

SHE Yes, and she's an awfully bad mother. Did you ever notice . . . when she's deciding between the two men, she doesn't give her children a thought. It's as if they don't exist.

HE Oh, that's not her fault. I think Shaw forgot he gave her children. What I object to is her personality.

SHE Yes! Isn't she revolting? I wonder if Shaw did it purposely. Maybe he despised her too.

HE If the woman I marry ever tries to manage me à la Madame Candida, I'll kick her down the stairs.

SHE (dimpling) Is that a threat?

HE It's a warning.

SHE (Softly) I'm not afraid. I'm going to be the kind of wife who looks up to her husband, the way I look up to you.

(AND SO ON)

To all appearances, a washrag has more spine than the girl who is plying Number 8, and many a big swaggering Tiger-cat has thought to insure himself everlasting supremacy by marrying the timid creature.

However, a little nibble of her own wedding cake gives a Mouse supernatural power, and all at once she becomes strong enough to clip her Tiger's claws, trim his whiskers, and swing him around by the tail.

———◆———

ELEVEN

The Formula

Formula 1: Generalissima

THE MAN who hates to make decisions, takes any action reluctantly, and is happiest when following instructions, is a perfect subject for Formula 1. A strong-minded girl, on recognizing this congenital subordinate, begins at once to play the role of Generalissima. She takes him by the hand and she takes him by the foot, and with magnificent self-confidence assumes full leadership.

He need never fear he has got the wrong seats for the wrong ballet on the wrong night, after using the wrong fork in the wrong restaurant and leaving a wrong tip. These details are taken care of by the Generalissima. It is she who decides where to go and when, where to eat and what, and murmurs advice to him as he vacillates with his hand over the silver.

And when he is faced with more important issues, he knows he need only ask—Should he change his job? Should he move to this apartment or that one? Should he fly or go by train? Should he fire his secretary? Should he shave again, or just use a little talc, and is it cold enough for a topcoat?—and a positive answer will be forthcoming. At no time does the Generalissima allow him to see in her the slightest hint of doubt or hesitation. She is ready always to tell him exactly what he must do.

So accustomed does he become to following her lead, that when the Generalissima says one day, "I think we'll get married in June—it's a much better month than July," he

automatically agrees, quite unaware that she has given the answer to a question he did not ask. Like an obedient soldier he marches briskly to the church, and presents her with the gold band that makes her his Commanding Officer for life.

Formula 2: The Woodpecker

Persistently, industriously, drilling away like a little woodpecker, the girl using Formula 2 works on the object of her desire, never allowing him to shut her out of his thoughts for more than twenty-four hours.

She sends him greeting cards on every occasion (and even on many a nonoccasion). She posts some sort of message or other to him daily *—affectionate, provocative, amusing, or at least friendly in content. These vary in length from one line to a long letter. "Last night was fun," or "Tomorrow is Ground-hog Day, thought you'd want to know," or "Remind me to tell you the dream I had about you," or "They say the temperature's going down. Please dress warmly," or "Are you taking care of your sacroiliac? I find myself worrying about you"—these are typical examples.

Before long the man, though he care not a jot for the sender, begins to look for some token of remembrance from her in each morning's mail. He comes to depend on it, to think it is his due. He feels disappointed, even hurt, if it is not forthcoming, and all day he is haunted by a sense of something lost or lacking.

The great advantage to this Formula is that it may be applied to any number of men simultaneously. A small

 This Formula is doubly effective when used on a philatelist. In such a case the envelope should always bear a commemorative, a special issue, a corner block, or some other item for his collection. How he will look forward, then, to hearing from you!

investment in stationery and postage will cover the cost of sending out ten, twenty, or thirty letters per day. And not too much time is involved, either, for if the writer chooses her words carefully she can send identical messages to all the names on her mailing list. The use of a typewriter or carbon paper, though economical and quick, is a mistake— the personal touch is so important.

Sometimes the Woodpecker sends a newspaper clipping —an article, or a cartoon, or a romantic bit of poetry. And sometimes she sends a little parcel containing an inexpensive souvenir (these are cheaper when bought in quantity), or a large parcel containing an assortment of goodies such as servicemen like to receive in camp.

Phone calls are substituted for mail once in a while, to impart some timely information or to ask a bit of masculine advice. But these are infrequent, for, unlike mail, a ringing phone insists on being answered, and having said "Hello," the recipient is obliged to carry on a conversation whether he wishes to or not—and no girl wants to be a pest.

A postal attack, however, is very unlikely to annoy a man, even one who is totally indifferent to the sender. If there are any who, month after month, never date her or thank her or give her some sign of encouragement, she rightly assumes they are impervious to this Formula or to her, and she strikes them off her list of prospects. She does not expect to hit the target with every paper dart she throws. She knows that if 30 per cent make a favorable response she is getting a better return than a mail order house.

The Woodpecker is efficient and unremitting. She relies on the theory that if she keeps peck-peck-pecking away, she may eventually peck, in someone's heart, a little hole for her to sneak into.

Formula 3: Cool, Cool Shoulder

Formula 3 is one that is brought into play by a girl when she sees that a man she has insulted or treated with indifference continues to seek her company. She turns and takes another look at him over a cool cool shoulder, and even though he has no appeal for her whatsoever, asks herself if she might not learn to tolerate him if he were her husband.

Should the answer be Yes, she does not change from cool to warm. She does not smile upon him if he is accustomed to her frowns. She is not cordial where she has been aloof. She knows it is her very haughtiness which makes her irresistible to him. He is one of those individuals whose perversity was so well described by Ovid: "What follows I flee; what flees I ever pursue."

His first proposal of marriage she rejects, the second or third she accepts with a half-hearted "Oh . . . all right. . . ." To keep him truly enslaved she holds him in such a torment of doubt that even as they stand at the altar he will wonder if she is going to say "I do" or "I don't."

My Aunt Lucy, who caught my Uncle Luke with this Formula, has maintained her unfriendly attitude throughout the thirty-seven years of their marriage, and he has never ceased to be her devoted lover. I am convinced that if she were suddenly to become a sweet, kind wife, Uncle Luke would lose all interest in her.

Formula 4: Little Girl Lost

This is the natural weapon of the dipsomaniac, nymphomaniac, kleptomaniac, and melancholiac, the neurotic, the psychotic, the underprivileged, the abused, and the defeated

—all those who have mistreated or been mistreated by Life.

Little Girl Lost does not pretend to be a normal, happy person. She confesses her weaknesses, advertises her misfortunes, gratefully accepts advice and help, makes brave plans for a better future, and weeps prettily on every masculine shoulder that is offered, clinging like a shipwrecked soul to a sturdy plank.

Very often one of those planks becomes a lifetime lifepreserver. For men are notoriously tenderhearted. While they may be ruthless about despoiling a girl who sits, dainty and smug, on a pedestal, they are wonderfully gentle with the pathetic creature they stumble over in the gutter. Literature and history testify that there is a kind of man who has a compulsion to rescue women in distress, even going so far as to marry a fallen member of Society. It is his pleasure to uplift what is degraded, to save, repair, and make over what is broken.

Sometimes the man who hungers for a waif, a harlot, or a misfit, is hoodwinked by a perfectly normal girl who can best be labeled Pseudo Little Girl Lost.

The Pseudo Little Girl Lost, unlike her genuinely pitiable sister, exaggerates any minor calamity she suffers, and even invents some where none exist. She will turn a little fuss with her mother into the autobiography of an unloved child, a cigarette cough becomes a mysterious lung ailment, a broken fingernail a sign of Fortune's prejudice against her.

Little Girl Lost, both the real and the Pseudo, gives her prey the feeling every time he leaves her, that the sad little creature he has just bidden Goodnight may be sticking her sad little head in the oven. More and more he becomes involved in her troubles and her problems. "She needs me," he tells himself. "She needs someone to protect her, and guide her, and love her. Poor helpless thing."

Blinded by tears of compassion, he does not see where she is leading him, and suddenly one day—Zzzzp! she snaps the lock. Another husband caught!

Formula 5: Fifiola

The Fifiola Formula is most commonly used by a genuine Fifiola (a female with a brain light as a soufflé), who has just enough intelligence to understand what she is, and to capitalize on it. Fifiola *features* her weakness instead of attempting to conceal it. She guilelessly admits a lack of ability to comprehend almost everything. Such phrases as

> I don't know how to. . . .
> But *this* is my left hand . . . or is it? . . . .
> Oh you're so clever. . . .
> I read it but I don't understand it. . . .
> Look, mine won't whistle. . . .

flow from her lips. Sometimes she laughs about her empty head, sometimes she cries—but she never pretends to be smarter than she is, and she never, never takes offense if she is corrected. Verily, she accepts criticism with such igenuous humility her critic feels impelled to hug and kiss her to prove he did not mean to be unkind.

The Fifiola has a marvelous appeal for men of low or mediocre intelligence, for with her they feel like mental giants. And even a brainy man can be charmed by a companion who never challenges his statements but looks with respect and wonder on his superior mentality.

How fondly, how tolerantly a man smiles upon the simple-minded girl. A charming child, a foolish, darling pet, he thinks. In her he sees a most desirable mate, one who will not correct him or catch him in a mistake, who will follow his instructions unquestioningly, who will believe her husband must be right though all the world insist that he is wrong.

He cannot foretell that after they are married she will lose respect for him. No man seems truly wise to his wife, and a Fifiola especially will ask herself, How smart can he really be, if he let himself be caught by silly little me?

Formula 6: Minerva

Oddly enough, the very same man who is charmed by a Fifiola is also susceptible to a Minerva—a girl with a well-

developed brain. For, like her backward sister, the intellectual miss who uses Number 6 makes him feel that she considers his mind better than hers—though in truth hers may be equal or superior to his.

This girl is equipped to meet the most erudite man on his own intellectual level. She is able to discuss with him any subject he finds interesting, whether it be poetry, politics, painting, philosophy, psychology, theology, anthropology, literature, theater, or opera. She manages always to introduce the subject of selective breeding, quoting frequently the words of Nobel prize winner, Dr. James Dewey Watson, whose field is genetics: "If you want to have an intelligent child you should have an intelligent wife."

Minerva has strong opinions of her own on everything, *But*—she is clever enough to know how far to carry a debate, and if she cannot lose it honestly, she loses it by cheating. She never exposes her adversary's ignorance or weakness on any point, and when they have got the fullest enjoyment out of tearing Ionesco or Sartre apart, she always in the end sees it his way. She is convinced. She is filled with admiration. She is excited by his brain and his brilliance.

And so, indeed, is he. He exults in her homage. He reflects that his intellectual attainments are wasted on the average female, and can be fully appreciated only by a brainy one. And he has some serious thoughts on Dr. Watson's advice.

Minerva never allows pride or willfulness to prod her into winning an occasional argument. She is not tempted to jeopardize the Great Victory for the sake of a few minor ones along the way. She well knows that Ionesco and Sartre, and Freud and Nietzsche and Shostakovitch and Picasso, and nuclear warfare and socialized medicine and the common market and capital punishment can be re-argued later when she is safely married to her opponent, and need no longer pamper his ego.

Formula 7: You're Mine!

Here is a Formula well suited to the self-confident girl who is not afraid to be brazenly impudent. At some unexpected moment she faces her victim and declares brightly, "I think I'll marry you!" It is quite a shock to a man the first time he hears these words. Some are so completely thrown off balance that they turn pale, and dumbly acquiesce. Some pick up their hats and run away. Others, indignantly, firmly, gently, or humorously declare themselves unwilling.

Whatever the tone of the rejection, the girl ignores it and continues her assault, speaking her lines lightly, jestingly. Here are some sample bits of persiflage:

"I always get what I want, and I've made up my mind—I want you."

"You're just what I'm looking for in a husband—why should I waste time looking further?"

"I'm not going to wait for some impossible oaf to ask *me*. Why can't the girl do the choosing?"

"You'll never get away—I'm going to hold on until you give in and marry me."

This is carried on quite openly, in the presence of friends, family, and strangers. If the man has any wit he will parry her sallies in the same vein. It makes for an amusing informal atmosphere—no one takes the girl entirely seriously, and no full-blooded male has ever objected to being openly wooed in this manner. In fact, the flattery of such an approach usually puts a man in a very happy state of mind, and he looks forward to being with a girl who is always tickling his vanity.

Formula 7 works particularly well with the kind of man

who is not outstanding in any way. It works even better on a lemon. With him there will not be the sparkling exchange of witty banter that makes this Formula so much fun, but as compensation the girl who sees in him a suitable mate will find his capture a comparatively simple matter. Dazed by the attention and the shameless pursuit, congratulating himself on having been found by someone who appreciates his worth, relieved of the pain of asking and the dread of being rejected, he quickly surrenders his bachelorhood to the first saucy girl who shouts, "You're mine!"

Formula 8: Peter and Wendy

Wendy is not really a Wendy and she does not go searching for a Peter Pan, but if she comes across one she is ready to net him with Formula 8.

Regardless of a Peter Pan's age (and sometimes he is not at all young) he is determined to remain eternally a boy. Capricious, irresponsible, full of whimsey, he capers through the adult world, disappearing like quicksilver from the sight of females who want to treat him like a man. But the girl who has a Wendy mask and a Wendy vocabulary—ah, she can fly with him to the Land of Lost Boys and he will never want her to leave him.

Here is a sample scene between a Peter and a Wendy. She is twenty three. He is thirty. She found him three weeks ago shopping in a toy store, helped him to decide on a new set of trains, and brought him home for ice cream and cookies.

(It is the very early morning of a summer day, and Wendy is roused from her sleep by the ringing of her doorbell.)

SHE (opening the door) Peter . . . Is anything wrong?

HE We're going on a picnic! Did you forget?

SHE But it's only seven o'clock. I told you to come at nine.

HE Well . . . but it's such a beautiful day, and. . . . (He shrugs, embarrassed)

SHE And you couldn't wait to get started. (She smiles indulgently) What a child you are! Come inside. Did you have breakfast?

HE (surprised) Breakfast? No. I forgot to.

SHE (Inspecting his hands) Wash your hands and wait for me in the kitchen while I go upstairs and calm Mother and Dad.

HE (guiltily) I woke them up. They'll hate me.

SHE Don't worry. I'll explain.

(When she joins him in the kitchen a little later, she discovers he has eaten half the layer cake she baked for the picnic, and doesn't want any breakfast. She scolds him gently, then:)

I have a surprise for you to take along on the picnic (she gives him a package that contains a kite). Why don't you look at it while I get dressed.

HE (following her to her bedroom) Should I open it right away, or try to guess what's in it?

SHE Try to guess. (She puts a finger on his lips) Quietly. You'll wake Mother and Dad.

HE (In a whisper as he goes toward her bed) Say, it is rather early. Why don't we snuggle in your bed while I unwrap my present? I love to snuggle.

SHE Oh Peter, you *are* a naughty boy. (putting her arms around him and kissing him warmly) You know very well we can't snuggle until we get one of those little certificates they give people at City Hall.

HE Oh, ——— City Hall.

130

SHE (Shaking her finger at him sternly) Stop using bad words.

HE (Wrestling with her) Come on. I have a present for you too. We'll open our things in bed and make believe it's Christmas.

SHE I hear Mother stirring. You'd better run downstairs. (He runs. When she is dressed and ready to leave she finds him assembling his kite on the parlor floor. She helps him gather it together, she combs his tousled hair, she ties his tie, she brushes his jacket, she asks him to check his pockets for money, car keys, handkerchief. At last they can depart. He opens the front door)

SHE Did you go to the bathroom?

(Grudgingly he turns around and goes back into the house)

While she waits for him she opens the gift he brought her. It is a book—A. A. Milne's *Now We Are Seven*. She gags slightly but recovers her equilibrium before he returns to her side. And how sweetly she smiles, stifling a wish that he break his leg as he jumps down the front steps like a ten year old, hurdles the hedge, and hops to his car. She prays that the neighbors are not watching and vows vengeance will be hers after they are married.

And indeed it is. No sooner does he utter the fateful words "I do," than she whisks him away from the Land of Lost Boys, and drops him with a thud in the midst of adult responsibilities. Quite often the sudden change from Wendy to Wifey will startle poor Peter out of his short pants and into maturity.

Formula 9: The Opportunist

A patient and far-sighted woman, The Opportunist worms her way into the family life of her married friends and relatives. She divides her attentions among as many of these as she is able and simply waits like a roulette player with chips on several numbers. Understanding, loyal, ready to help in any crisis, what a comfort she is when the Grim Reaper strikes down a wife and creates a widower.

She is there—a familiar face, a helping hand—to see the bereaved man through. How grateful he is for this Dear Old Friend who shares his memories with him, knows how much sugar he takes in his tea, and how much starch in his shirts, and provides female companionship at a time when he could not decently look for it elsewhere. Gradually The Opportunist takes upon herself all the duties of the departed one and so smooth is the transition that he is hardly aware that a new partner has been substituted for the old one.

The only difference—which he cannot but notice— is that the Old Friend is much nicer to him than the Old Wife ever was. She is indulgent, uncritical, and eager to spoil him. Elated by his good fortune, this unexpected second chance, he weds her, looking forward to a new kind of life with this new kind of wife. Ha ha.

TWELVE

———◆———

Love Potions

Variation A: Fire and Tears

THIS VARIATION is used by the militant girl who is willing to employ forceful measures to capture an indifferent or obstinate man. Having decided that he is precisely what she wants, and that no one else will do, she woos him without subterfuge, without coyness, and without shame, no matter how strenuously he resists her.

She will stir up the embers of a finished friendship, or, making all the overtures, start one that is slow in getting started. She frankly tells the chosen one she loves him, and constantly testifies to it with gifts and little attentions and invitations and protestations, and tears and promises

133

and passionate declarations. No matter how many times he sends her on her way, she will not abandon her cause. Always she reappears and continues the campaign. She loves him! she claims. She will never give him up! She cannot! And what a good wife she will be to him! And what a good mother to their children! And so forth and so on.

Some who use this Variation of the Love Potion make hysterical scenes in the presence of rivals. Or go so far as to threaten suicide, claiming they cannot go on living without the man they love. Others bully a parent or sister or former boy friend into pleading for them.

The man who likes turbulent seas and windswept mountain peaks will enjoy the whirlpool of emotion which is constantly whipped up by this girl. What a wealth of material is here for dramatic and tragic performances. Often enough a victim with theatrical leanings is carried away by the excitement of it all and, tempted to play the hero, finds himself acting out the inevitable climax at his own wedding.

Even a quiet reserved chap cannot help but be moved by the tumult. He shifts from a feeling of annoyance to one of gratification. He is flattered by such persistent devotion, and is smitten by a sense of responsibility toward the woman in whom he has inspired it. If he is soft-hearted he will be touched by it. If he is soft-headed he will be overwhelmed by it. Sometimes he finds himself actually growing fond, in a patronizing way, of the spunky little thing who wants him so desperately. And sometimes, exhausted by the relentless attack, and taken in by the promises, he will capitulate.

I have seen strong men go down gasping, "Why doesn't she leave me alone! I had my heart set on a tall blonde! Oh gad! I can't fight it any more!"

134

While we applaud the success of the girl, we at the same time feel a reluctant pity for the man she drugs into submission with Variation A, for he almost always has the embarrassing task of explaining his about-face to the friends and relatives who have heard him shout again and again, "That girl is crazy. I wouldn't marry her if she were the last female on earth!"

Variation B: Bittersweet

There is a segment of the male population which is considered unsuitable for husband material. Some girls, however, do not share the popular point of view. They maintain

—That so long as the Male/Female ratio is as it is, we cannot afford to waste even one male, regardless of his inadequacies.

—That a lack of masculinity does not preclude a talent for domesticity.

—And that this much-maligned variety of Man can be a most entertaining companion, an undemanding husband, and a devoted father.

To their critics these girls quote Stratford: "The nest of the weaver-bird (*ploceidae*) seems queer to the starling, but it is a nest nonetheless and the weaver-bird is content with it."

It is usually a girl of delicate temperament who puts forth these arguments. Though she longs for a home and family of her own, she lacks the animal spirits necessary for coping with the friction and the wear and tear, the jealousies and the passions that distinguish the average marriage. A regular man is a bit too rough for her.

Carrying a full flagon of Love Potion, Variation B, she sets out to find an appropriate subject, a search which requires patience and perception—not because males of this type are scarce, but because they are elusive and not always recognizable, and they do not, moreover, welcome every offer of feminine friendship.

When one is found, the gentle huntress pours out on him quantities of tender affection, and charms him with her elegance and sweet ways. So chic, so sophisticated, so understanding is she, so persuasively does she present the advantages of living behind the façade of conventional marriage, that the trusting fellow is won over. Assured by her every action that he is safe, he puts his hand in hers, and like two nice children they pledge their troth.

Only later, saddled with babies and mortgages, does he discover they are not just "playing house." He is as much a slave as any other husband.

Variation C: Milk and Honey

Man is proud and believes he should be loved for himself alone. It offends his vanity when a girl expects him to spend money on her entertainment. Moreover, it wounds him in the purse. He returns from a date, empties his pockets, totals up the evening's costs and weighs them against the evening's profits—and more often than not he asks himself if he really had his money's worth.

How pleased he is when he finds a girl who does not head for taxis, pause in front of flower shops, gaze in every jeweler's window, or pull toward expensive restaurants. And when she not only asks for naught, but goes so far as to spend *her* money on *him*, he is enchanted.

The girl who brews this potion rarely lets a week go by without presenting the chosen one with some little gift. Once it is a tie that "just matches his eyes," then it is a book she knows he is looking for, and then a special pastry he likes, and a band for his watch to replace the one that broke, and a gadget for his kitchen, and a something for his office, and a sweater she knitted with her own little needles.

If these samples of her generosity do not evoke sufficient gratitude she gives gifts of greater value. Though a girl of good breeding will not accept expensive presents from an admirer, a man will accept anything without embarrassment. In truth, he would feel, and look, perfectly silly if he sent back a costly movie camera, for example, saying "It breaks my heart to turn this down, darling, but it wouldn't be proper to accept it from you."

By a planned program of giving, a girl can play cunningly on masculine emotions. A tennis racquet, a fine dog, a beautiful horse,* always catch the victim by surprise. And

Few men will take a horse from a girl and then not marry her.

if the donor spends more than she can afford, this is the kind of extravagance that touches a man deeply.

Sometimes he responds with boyish greediness. He takes and takes and gives nothing in return. But since each meeting with his Lady Bountiful holds the promise of a new surprise, he can never see enough of her. All this leads inevitably to the day when in answer to his customary "What did you bring me?" she snaps open a little square box inside of which there nestles a ring. As a matter of habit he takes it, with kisses of thanks, and only after she has clamped it on his finger with a vow of everlasting fidelity, and ordered announcements of their betrothal does he realize what has been done to him.

A more openhanded type of man is inclined to feel indebted if he accepts so much as a bag of gumdrops, and he can hardly refrain from reciprocating. For every gift he receives he gives one in return. Caught in this give-and-take he is led by imperceptible steps from harmless souvenirs to an exchange of more incriminating items until the day comes when he has no choice but to give a ring for a ring.

The outcome is not always so felicitous. Rings have been

refused, returned, or run away with. (One man who found himself with a ring on his hand recovered from his astonishment quickly and evened up matters by presenting the girl with a one year voyage around the world.) But by and large, the girl who lavishly ladles out Variation C, has a fair chance to win a husband, and nothing to lose but money.

Variation D: Manna

It is an inspiring sight to see a girl so determined to win a mate she will wade through the mire to find him. This valiant creature fastens on to some disheartened fellow who has been batted about by unkind gods, and tries to drag him out of his slough. Generously she soaks him in her Love Potion, a sticky mess of tenderness and love and hope and grit, which has been known to work wonders. She takes away his bottle and gives him her warm hand in its place. She feeds his undernourished ego. She lifts his sorry soul. She props up his chin.

One must admire a girl who forages in the junk heap for a husband. Hers is not an easy task. Quite often the bit of debris she would salvage does not respond properly. Unable or unwilling to hold his chin up, he slumps out of her grasp, flopping back into a comfortable state of collapse. But sometimes her determined efforts are rewarded. I have seen a tenderhearted lass pick up some patently worthless piece of manhood, stand him on his feet, brush him off, drench him in the magic ingredients, and turn him into a useful member of society, capable of drudging his life away in her service. Such a girl deserves success!

THIRTEEN

Spellbinders

Spellbinder 1: Gold

WEALTH IS relative, and that which has the weight of a fortune in Chimney Corners becomes light as pin money on Park Avenue. The Golden Girl, therefore, may be a world-famous heiress, the only child of a banker, the widow of a heavily insured shopkeeper, or the winner of an Irish Sweepstake. According to the standard of her own particular circle, she is the possessor of an enviable portion of wealth.

Some rich girls are self-conscious. They are ever on the defensive against fortune hunters, ever fearful that they are wooed only for their wealth. But others glory in their riches and use it unashamedly as a Spellbinder. They publicize it, flaunt it, dangle it like bait, and artfully gild the gold—all in the manner of a Beauty who shows off her charms.

These Golden Girls say quite reasonably, "Does a beauty feel insulted or disillusioned because she is loved for her beauty? Not at all. And neither do I when I am loved for my Money. Both assets are simply accidents of Fate." And they boast that their Accident is the better one—that Beauty fades and vanishes, whereas Money, if properly handled, increases and flowers over the years; that a man may grow tired of his wife's beauty, but no man ever gets tired of his wife's money; and that those who are enticed by gold are practical, ambitious men, far more desirable as husbands than the romantic, superficial ones who place so much importance on physical beauty.

At the outset the girl who is using this Spellbinder concentrates her efforts on capturing a husband who is worthy

of her—i.e., worth as much as she is. (Or more.) If she cannot negotiate a profitable merger, she takes her money and shops around for the very best man she can buy.

When she finds one to her liking she shows him her assets; she lets him clip her coupons, run his fingers through her safe deposit box, play with her dividends, and advise her on her investments. She lets him experience all the heady sensations of wealth, and when she hints that everything she has will be put in the hands of the man who marries her, he is caught.

Actually, the Golden Girl has no intention of giving up one iota of her power. She may generously allow her husband to share her luxurious way of life, but no matter how piteously he tugs at her purse strings, she holds them in a relentless grip. For she well knows that with her gold she captured him and with her gold she will chain him to her side forevermore.

Certain professions have an aura of glamour about them. Ordinary men are dazzled when they come into contact with an actress or an opera singer or a lady psychiatrist or a tightrope walker.

The girl who has a glamorous profession knows it is a Spellbinder—she herself is bewitched by it—and she quickly notifies every man she meets that she is what she is. Modesty is of no value, for these special girls seldom look different from other girls, and if they did not proclaim their glamorous status no one would know of it. That is why a model will go about with a magazine open to the page that has her picture on it, a lady doctor will appear at cocktail parties wearing her stethoscope like a necklace, and an aviatrix will refuse to step foot out of the house without her parachute.

If simple visual advertisements are impractical they will employ oblique ones. The *non sequitur* does not frighten them. A reference to Spanish Omelette is a perfect opening for "Oh! I shall never forget the first time I sang Carmen." A funeral is reason enough for a writer to speak of her deadline. A case of Scotch provides a lady barrister with a chance to inform all listeners that she is handling a case of mayhem.

The glamorous ones lose no opportunity to titillate the masculine ear with choice gossip and intimate references to the great. Men are fascinated by the girl who can casually say, "Onassis was so sweet to us. He invited the whole cast on his yacht after the opening," or "When the Shah heard we were stranded in Tangiers he sent three Rolls Royces to transport us to the palace," or "She *is* beautiful, but bald as an egg, you know. Her wig maker told my understudy."

It is not necessary for a girl to be successful in her field. Unless he is a celebrity worshipper, a man does not measure worth by such standards. If he meets an actress he does not ask whether she is a star or an extra, whether she is on Broadway, or Off-Broadway, or still in Dramatic School. It is enough for him that she is a part of the magic world of Theater. Similarly, a Writer or a Sculptress may have earned the right to label herself thus, simply by renting a room in Greenwich Village. For him it is enough. She is his passport into a more exciting and more meaningful world, a cultish, exclusive, very special realm which does not open its gates to unimportant outsiders unless they are married to insiders.

The girl who uses this Spellbinder gives her subject no hint of what the future holds for him. If she is sated with the rigors and uncertainties of her calling, she is careful not to reveal until after the wedding that, regardless of her bridegroom's wishes, she is determined to retire and devote herself to making him happy.

Equally secretive is the acrobat, singer, dancer, musician, model, actress, news correspondent, doctor, etc., etc., who is in love with her career. Only after the ceremony does it become evident that she is always on call for auditions, rehearsals, out of town tours, professional conferences, seminars, foreign assignments, and emergency operations; that when she does come home she comes with sore feet and weary bones—exhausted, tense, keyed up over a success, weeping over a disappointment, or hysterical because of a rival's triumph; that her attention is focused on her work and she is too tired or too busy to partake of the very festivities that lured him in the first place.

How sad.

Spellbinder 3: Prestige

Men who have social aspirations, who crave the deference of their peers, who wish for an eminence they cannot attain with their own resources, are drawn to the girl with a well-known name.

If she is a famous author, tennis player, or pianist, or the daughter, granddaughter, niece, by-blow, or mistress of a famous author, tennis player, or pianist; if she has a title or is in any way connected with someone who has a title; * if her family name is known everywhere for its association with beer, pills, munitions, or finance; if she has

With what pride does a prestige-seeker say of his wife, "Ellie was once married to Lord Forsoothe, you know."

even a remote claim to a distinguished ancestor; if, in other words, she can be introduced as a Somebody, instantly identifiable, she is a girl who can win the socially ambitious man simply by pointing * to her prestige.

The usual repertoire of compliments, gifts, sweet manners, false promises, and loving ways are not employed by her. Her Prestige seems to diminish if she tries in any way to please him, whereas it is enhanced when she behaves as though she has conferred an extraordinary favor by granting him the honor of her company.

The girl who is equipped with Spellbinder 3 does not let her victim forget who she is. After she has given up her Big Name in exchange for his Little Name, she is inclined to preserve a certain distance between herself and her husband. But the snob who seeks a socially superior wife respects such distinctions, and he will be the first to acknowledge her right to be condescending toward him, and even toward the children she bears him.

Spellbinder 4: Aphrodite

This Spellbinder is reserved for shy or inexperienced or unsophisticated men whose natural instincts are shackled by fear—fear of being rebuffed, fear of evoking laughter instead of sighs, fear of not doing the right thing in the right way. This lack of confidence is not apparent to everyone. It may hide behind the forbidding exterior of an overbearing professor or bill collector, and those who are at his mercy never suspect they are dealing with a timid lover. But Aphrodite can always tell.

 A girl with prestige need not be afraid to point. She is above the necessity of observing rules of etiquette designed for commonplace people.

Widow, divorcée, worldly lady, or unconventional gamin, she is one who is wise in the ways of love. She recognizes on sight her counterpart, Mr. A or B, the man who is at home in Aphrodite's temple and is well versed in its rituals, its beauties, and its shams. And just as quickly does she recognize those who loiter at the portals, not daring to enter, waiting hopefully to be led inside.

When Aphrodite holds out her hand to the Timid Lover, he seizes it gratefully. In humble adoration he follows wherever she leads, and listens enraptured to her siren song. She makes veiled allusions to her countless adventures, hints at pleasures too exquisite to be described, and gives assurance that there are no delights she cannot dispense. What promise she offers of marital bliss, what pictures she paints of a lifetime of orgiastic revelry.

The prudent Aphrodite will permit her victim no more than a sampling of a few well-chosen embraces. She does not give herself until after he has given himself as a sacrifice on the altar of her relative, Hymen.

The more carefree Aphrodite withholds nothing. She invites her follower to participate in the final ritual— sometimes only once in order to tantalize him and force him into complete subjugation—sometimes often, in order to enslave him, in which case he becomes so addicted to her ceremonies that he cannot go back to an existence without them.

Enthralled by the prospect of living in the very temple of the love-goddess he signs himself over to her. Too late does he discover that he has sold himself into bondage and is obliged, like any husband, to work so hard to pay the landlord and the hairdresser and the grocer that he is too tired to revel with his goddess as he had dreamed. And oh how nerve-racking it is for him to wonder if in his absence his Aphrodite receives other worshippers, according to the custom of ancient deities.

Spellbinder 5: The Enchanted Circle

Nothing is more heartwarming than the atmosphere that prevails in the bosom of a happy family. The mutual trust and admiration, the gaiety, the good humored chaffing, the solidarity, the insularity—all combine to make an Enchanted Circle, an exclusive club that every man longs to join. It is too ideal to be real—the perfect love and understanding between Mother and Father, parents and children, sisters and brothers.

Why do they do it? Why do they pretend? To aggravate neighbors and friends? To arouse envy? To prove themselves superior to families riddled with boredom and split by squabbles?

No one can explain why the members of these "happy" households conspire to give the impression that Peace and Joy reign in their homes. It is done without rehearsal and without spoken agreement. The group simply responds with spontaneous unity to the stimulus of an outsider's presence. Before an audience, feuds are temporarily suspended, insults are exchanged only in jest, tensions, jealousies, and dark undercurrents are hidden away.*

Whatever the reason behind this show, they fool everyone, or almost everyone. Men who come from homes where the same charade is regularly performed are sometimes skeptical. But to the orphan, or the exile from a foreign land, or the fellow who comes from a family that is frankly disagreeable, the Enchanted Circle is irresistible and the girl who has this Spellbinder in her possession exposes him to it with confidence. She invites the chosen man to share the intimate festivities of her Wonderful Family—birthdays, anniversaries, Christmas dinners, etc. More and more she draws him into the embrace of her loving clan, surrounding him with companionship and jollity.

Debilitated by the emotional security of group life, and fearful lest it be taken away from him, he vows the vows that give him in-law status and make him a bona fide, permanent member of the Enchanted Circle. After he has recovered from the initial shock of seeing the performers as they really are, the bridegroom invariably joins the act, and loyally upholds the tradition of the "Happy Family."

 There are married couples, too, who like to baffle everyone by behaving like romantic lovers.

———•◆•———

FOURTEEN

How to Design
Your Own Method

It is possible that none of the foregoing Methods seems exactly right for you or for the man at hand. Or you may object to following easy, oft-trodden paths. In either event, I suggest you create a well-thought-out Method of your own, using the following fundamental materials:

Sex   *   Comfort   *   Flattery

Sex. It is impossible to blueprint the use of Sex and I can only say that this element must be handled with the most delicate finesse. It is quite different from Comfort or Flattery, where if one is too generous or a bit careless no great harm is done.

Comfort. Unless a man feels positively repelled by her, he will be unable to tear himself away from a girl who surrounds him with comforts. Be lavish with your attentions. Coddle him. Pamper him. Do not be afraid that he will become spoiled. He will learn quickly enough after marriage that he must shift for himself. And is it not justice that he be allowed for a short period to loll on a bed of flowers in exchange for the years of slavery that lie ahead? Not only must you make the courted man comfortable. You must avoid making him *un*comfortable. Do not send him on errands in bad weather, insist that he spend time with people he dislikes, correct his manners, disparage his friends, laugh at his haircuts, try to manage his finances, or scoff at his opinions. A girl with any degree of self-control can hold herself in check and make a man's life pleasant until after the wedding.

Flattery. Flattery is more than a string of pretty words: How big you are! What a marvelous sense of humor you have! I do like the shape of your fingernails. Your insight is remarkable. Etcetera, etcetera. Not that such bonbons are ineffective. Sour men grow sweet, gruff men gentle, strong men weak, when honeyed words are poured into their ears. But actions are more potent than spoken compliments. You can flatter a man by the way you look at him, by the kind of presents you give him, by the manner in which you hang up his coat and react to his kisses, by the tender pat you give his dog. Indeed there is hardly an act you perform which cannot convey to him your admiration.

To the fundamentals, Sex, Comfort, and Flattery, you must add your own magic ingredient, some tangible or intangible which will sink into him like a Limerick hook, so that it will be more painful for him to pull away from you than to go where you lead him.

Every one of the 33 Methods here described was once designed by some enterprising girl, or by a number of designers working together. Some were evolved out of necessity, some out of desperation, some out of meanness, some out of love. Perhaps the one you create will be so original and so effective that it will become Method 34 and be brought into universal use.

Good luck!

FIFTEEN

For the
Career-minded Girl

SOME GIRLS are happy-go-lucky. They play Doctor, Lawyer, Indian Chief, Rich Man, Poor Man, Beggarman, Thief, and cheerfully they take whatever button falls to them. Other girls know exactly what they want and they go after it in a businesslike fashion. Still others are quite sure of what they want but do not know how to set about getting it.

It is to the girls in the third category that this chapter is addressed.

For the girl who wants a man of medicine

The Doctor is considered a prime catch. This is not surprising since the average mean income of medical men in the United States is second only to that of industrialists. And actually, doctors are better off than this statistic would indicate, for many of them have secret little safes into which they stuff, tax free, every other cash fee.

There are a number of ways to go about catching a doctor.

Program One. Enroll in a Medical School.

Nobody has a better chance of winning a Man Doctor than a Lady Doctor.

However, you need not work through four grueling years and actually earn your own M.D. if all you desire is a husband with an M.D. You can get one of these in your first year. It is as easy as shooting fish in a barrel, for the enrollment in medical colleges is extravagantly, excessively male.* So favorable is the sex ratio that every female student who faints over her first cadaver may reasonably expect to be revived by twenty male classmates. How marvelous to live in a Society where the absence of prejudice against the female enables her to pursue a medical student right in the classroom.

I advise that you select a promising student with good grades. The wife of my druggist married him while he was in medical school, never suspecting that he would flunk out. He had hoped to be a heart specialist, and for this foolishly romantic reason she chose him over an A student who liked nothing better than diseases of the liver. The rejected suitor is now a big stomach man and, in an ironic aftermath, the squeamish lady who would not have him, pays him high fees to treat the ulcers she developed fretting over her mistake.

 The same thing is true of schools for dentists, optometrists, pharmacists, and veterinarians.

Program Two. Insinuate Yourself Into the Life of a Medical School. If you are unable to meet the requirements for enrollment (and, alas, few of us have brains good enough for that) you can nevertheless manage to enjoy almost as many benefits as the matriculated girl. Take up residence in the vicinity of your chosen school.*

Be selective. Do not assume that one medical school is as good as another. To illustrate: Cornell Medical College is a highly respected institution, but (and this I regret) it must be marked N.G. It is, by my standards, worthless, since it is situated in girl-glutted Manhattan. You want to be at least 40 miles away from any city. A small college town, quiet, remote, is ideal, for in such a place the student body is constantly tormented by the scarcity of females.

Get as close as you can, as often as you can, to these hungry men. Always eat in the college cafeteria, even if you have no business being on the campus at all. Haunt the library. Attend every lecture, church activity, sporting event, dance, discussion group, and club meeting that takes place. If evicted, leave quietly, but do not hesitate to try again and again and again. Your face will become familiar, and after a while nobody will question your right to be present. In one way or another you will come to know a goodly number of students † and their professors on whom you can use your Lures, Traps, and other Methods.

Trap 6, the Helpmeet, is most effective in this context. An impecunious youth can hardly decline an offer of bed,

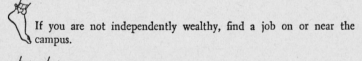

If you are not independently wealthy, find a job on or near the campus.

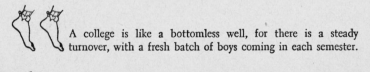

A college is like a bottomless well, for there is a steady turnover, with a fresh batch of boys coming in each semester.

board, and spending money through the hard years of study and internship. And an ambitious girl will not hesitate to marry and support such a man for five or six or eight years. It is a blue chip investment.

Program Three. Attach Yourself to a Hospital. It may be that neither Program One nor Program Two are feasible. As a poor third, you might consider a career as nurse or hospital technician. This will certainly throw you into the company of doctors. However, in the wake of every single doctor you will find a pursuing horde of females.* The licensed M.D., the titled man who struts through a hospital, smiling like a sultan on his nurses, placing a benign hand on his female patients, pinching here, patting there, juggling the countless invitations that come his way—how much more difficult to catch this lion in the heyday of his power than when he was a mere cub, locked away in the classroom, yearning for female companionship.

Still, it has been done. If knock-down drag-out competition does not frighten you, by all means become a nurse. If you fail to get a doctor you will at least be in a worthwhile profession, one which gives you constant access to a vast variety of males, many of them flat on their backs.

According to the *American Journal of Nursing*, as reported in the New York *Times*, November 4, 1962, marriage is one of the chief reasons for the shortage of nurses. To quote: "The recruitment for staff vacancies is a perpetual race with Cupid." One hospital director complains: "Over half . . . are married within a year after graduation and nearly all are married within two or three years."

 Doctors are in such great demand that even their paying customers find it hard to attract their attention. A dear friend of mine, felled by pneumonia, was dead and buried a whole week before her doctor could find time to visit her.

A word of caution before leaving the subject of Doctors

There is a possibility that in the not too distant future the Doctor will lose his exalted status, his social prestige, his financial superiority, and that he will become the mere servant of humanity. The specter of Socialized Medicine haunts the entire profession. If strong doctors turn pale when it is mentioned, one may well imagine how sick it makes their wives. Before embarking on your difficult quest, ask yourself this question: How would I feel if I woke up one morning and found that my husband, The Doctor, had been by decree transformed into a civil service employee?

For the girl who wants a man of science

While the M.D. may soon become passé in the marriage mart, the Scientist is definitely *le dernier cri*. Mathematicians, Engineers, Physicists, Chemists, these are the men of today and of tomorrow.

Program One. This is the same as Program One for Doctors. NOTE. For every girl student in Engineering there are more than 300 boy students!!!!

Program Two. Here again we follow the corresponding program for Doctors.

Program Three. Unlike the Doctor, the Scientist can be captured after he has his degree just as easily as before. He is not lifted into the excitement of hospital life and eager female arms when he finishes his studies. On the contrary, he is very often sent off to a research laboratory,

158

an austere institution, located far from the centers of fun and frolic, and almost destitute of females.

It is a source of wonder to me that the entire maiden population does not rush posthaste to these hives which dot the nation from coast to coast and swarm with lonely, high-salaried men. The addresses are not secret. Simply go to the library and leaf through the technical magazines such as *Physics Today, Industrial Research, Nucleonics, Scientific American,* and others of that nature. You will find want ads galore for scientists of every type, and each advertisement will give you the information you are looking for. It is good practice to write to the various personnel managers and inquire about a job for yourself before making a final decision, for you will want to give preference to the company that takes you inside its walls and permits you to rub elbows all the livelong day with the very kind of man you want to marry.

In choosing your base of operations, pray, resist the lure of big cities. Do not turn up your nose at names such as Almagordo, New Mexico; Los Alamos, New Mexico; Richland, Washington; Arco, Idaho; Oak Ridge, Tennessee; Corning, New York. It is in out-of-the-way towns like these that you are likely to find conditions comparable to those which Great-Grandmama enjoyed in pioneer days—those golden days when every female was a rare and sought-after prize.

For the girl who wants a man of war

With all the nations of the world singing their war songs at the top of their voices, the Military Man has come into his own as a figure of importance. Furthermore, because of the advances in nucleonics and the marvelous things the scientists are doing with peroxide, the Military Man has become a highly desirable mate. No longer can his work be classified as "too hazardous" now that civilians enjoy as little safety as fighting men in time of war. Nor can it be said that the future of the Military Man is a limited one. There is no limit to how far he can go. Outer space today—tomorrow the Moon.

Naturally, every girl would like to be married to an Astronaut, to ride through cheering throngs beside her hero-husband, to shake the hand of the President, to lunch with the First Lady, to be interviewed and photographed, and envied by her friends. But everybody knows Astronauts cannot be captured; they all have wives.*

Since there is no such thing as a Bachelor-Astronaut you will have to trust to luck that the Military Man you marry will eventually become one of the chosen ones. Do your best to catch someone who is obviously good Astronaut material—someone who is tall, intelligent, a good talker, with fine teeth, an engaging TV personality, and charming parents. (Goodness, such a man would make a darling husband even if he did not achieve your ambition.)

Since the Astronaut is the rarest creature in the world, it would be unwise to put all your hopes into getting one. There are good husbands to be found in every branch of the Service, as well as promise of a life filled with travel, band music, natty uniforms, special discounts, and predictable promotions.

Program One. Program One, as outlined for Doctors, cannot be applied to the Man of War, since it is impossible for a girl, no matter how well-qualified she may be, to enroll

---

It is interesting to note that our government has never entrusted a spaceship to an unmarried man.

at Annapolis or West Point or the Air Force Academy—
an inequity which I hope will one day be corrected.

Program Two. Number 2 for Doctors does not lend itself
readily to the Military, since marriage is forbidden to the
undergraduates of all three of the great war schools. To
wait on the outskirts, hoping to hold someone's interest
until his four years are up, and then gamble on being able
to march him to the altar between the day he gets his com-
mission and the day he is shipped out to his first assign-
ment, seems to me a highly impractical procedure.

Program Three. Become a WAC or a WAVE or a WAF.
There was a time, not too long ago, when the idea of a
girl being admitted into man's private world of guns and
bugles seemed like a naughty dream. Now your government
has thrown open to you the doors of the sanctum sanc-
torum, and you are invited, yea coaxed, to enter and take
your pick of the country's fighting men. This, in brief, is
what the USAF Recruiting Service says:

> Few careers provide the excitement, varied experi-
> ence, pride and deep gratification of service to
> country as does membership in the USAF. It is a
> challenging career laced with the unexpected and
> the unusual.

What they do not mention, probably because it is too obvious, is the glorious Male/Female ratio.

If you hate discipline or do not look nice in uniform, then
you should remain a civilian. Go to live near an army or
naval station, an air force or minuteman missile base. Again
I counsel you: Look for the undeveloped areas—the isolated
naval base, the lonely army post. Go to Great Falls, Mon-

161

tana. Go to Okinawa or Guam. Or go to the NATO nations where our boys are so lonesome they are marrying the natives.

For the girl who wants a man with a million

You will probably be surprised to learn that there are in these United States only 17,000 millionaires (give or take a few). Finding them is quite a problem. Whereas it is easy to become associated with a multitude of medical students, or a multitude of engineers, or a multitude of military men, it is a rather complicated matter to become associated with a multitude of millionaires.

Neither Program One nor Program Two, as employed in previous categories is useful here. Almost without exception the millionaires found in college are only embryo millionaires, the sons of millionaires, and even if you were content to try for one of these you would soon discover that they are far too difficult to locate. For in our great democracy the heirs of millionaires are not conveniently gathered together in exclusive colleges, but are indiscriminately mingled with the sons of ordinary men in colleges throughout the land. It is evident that a special program is needed for the pursuit of millionaires, as even Program Three must be modified extensively.

Special Program A. Let us take first things first. Do you know how to recognize a millionaire? Can you tell him apart from the comfortably rich, the hanger-on, the crasher, the climber, or the spendthrift? The millionaire wears no uniform or other distinguishing marks,* carries no certifi-

 There is a handful of names which are synonymous with great fortunes but even these names are not to be taken as proof positive. I once had a shoe salesman at Bonwit's named Ford. And it is well-

cate, has no title, and is never identified for what he is. People will say, "This is Mr. Jones, the botanist," or "This is Mr. Jones, the composer," but nobody ever says, "This is Mr. Jones, the millionaire." Mr. Jones himself will rarely say, "I am a millionaire."

In any event it is not safe to rely on a verbal statement from anyone where so much money is involved. What you need and should have is an authenticated list giving the full name and address of each and every millionaire in the country. Lists of this nature can be obtained from one of the several companies which make a business of compiling them. I recently priced one at Boyd's City Dispatch, Inc. (373 Broadway, New York City), and was quoted a figure of $600. If this seems too dear, remember, it is all part of the overhead and one must allow for this in any financial enterprise. Moreover, if you break down the figures you will find that 17,000 millionaires for $600 comes to only 3½ cents apiece.

Should you be willing to try for a ½-millionaire (and one ought not be inflexible about demanding a whole one) you may purchase a list which reveals the names and addresses of the 45,000 ½-millionaires in the United States. This gives you a wider field to work in.

Do try to fit at least one if not both lists into your budget. You might consider bringing a few other girls in on the venture, thus cutting the cost. Or perhaps you can borrow a list. In some way or another you must manage to get your hands on one. It will be invaluable to you in your quest, serving as credit index and as guide map.

Study your list. Make a geographic analysis of it. Select an area in which there is an inviting concentration of mil-

---

known that the DuPonts keep the young men of the family in an almost impoverished condition, insisting that they make their own way, as the commoners do (albeit within their private empire).

lionaires. Memorize the names of those millionaires. Now, plunge yourself into their midst. Go to their resorts, and to their summer and winter colonies. Join their country clubs, and their yacht clubs, and their charitable organizations. In short, play in the playgrounds of the rich.

Special Program A is a Champagne Program, and requires a certain amount of capital. It will work best for the girl who herself has some means—and indeed it is usually just that kind of girl who feels the greatest need for a millionaire, and who, I might add, will know how to make the best use of him when she gets him. However, there are poor girls, too, who have a genuine love and appreciation of money. The poor girl who feels she must have a millionaire should borrow, or induce a friend or relative to provide her with a grubstake. Failing this, she can try Special Program B.

Special Program B. Proceed exactly as you would under Special Program A, with this difference—You must work, not play, among the millionaires. It is not folklore but fact that millionaires marry hatcheck girls, waitresses, secretaries, entertainers, reporters, and nurses. If you have the necessary skills, you might do well as a servant in a private home. You have undoubtedly heard about the girl who, not too long ago, came to America, found employment in the household of one of the world's richest men, and worked her way up very quickly from domestic to daughter-in-law. This brilliant feat, performed by a big, plain, wholesome girl, should serve as an inspiration to every ambitious female.

The programs laid out in this chapter do not purport to win the desired man for you. What they will do is provide the most propitious, and in some cases foolproof, conditions under which to use the Methods of your choice on men in the career of your choice.

SIXTEEN

Girls! Fasten Your Chastity Belts!

IT SOMETIMES happens that a girl becomes so engrossed in working out the Method she has chosen, she forgets to be on guard against the sly tricks employed by men. After all, the man you are trying to capture is not a neutral, senseless target. He has his own objective—to take from you, without forfeit, that which you want him to pay for with his very name. You must constantly bear in mind the fact that you and he are working at cross purposes.

In this conflict your strongest armor is the conviction that

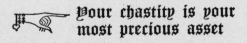 **Your chastity is your most precious asset**

Although man implicitly acknowledges and upholds this evaluation, he behaves, particularly in his bachelor days, as though a woman's chastity is a useless encumbrance. By means of specious logic he can reduce it to an absurdity. An innocent feminine plea like, "Please don't ask me to give myself to you," is answered with arrant sophistry.

"Give? GIVE?" he chides. "A woman does not 'give' herself. Between a man and a woman there is no such thing as giving or taking. There is simply a coming together, a mutual impulse to make each other happy." But even as he says this he knows there is no truth in it, for

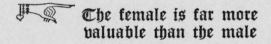

The female is far more valuable than the male

and there can be no simple coming together by two people of such disparate worth.

Man acknowledges woman's superior value over and over again, by supporting our marriage and divorce laws and our social customs, even though they operate in his disfavor. These laws and customs are pervaded by the spirit of

THE DOUBLE STANDARD

which provides different sets of rules to govern the conduct of men and of women. Inherent in this difference is the belief that the female body is sacrosanct, the male body rather ordinary and of no special worth. (It is difficult to ascertain exactly how this principle was evolved, but I am sure it is based on a very beautiful and spiritual idea.)

In supporting the Double Standard, men display a humility that is touching. Let us examine for a moment the attitude they have toward Virginity.

A man who is a virgin is an object of laughter or speculation. His virginity has no value—it is in fact a source of embarrassment. He tries to lose it as quickly as possible, caring not one whit who takes it from him, just so long as he rids himself of it. Nobody, least of all the man, thinks he is giving away anything of the slightest consequence.

How directly opposite is the value of Virginity in a woman! An object of veneration, extolled in song and legend and universally admired, it is ideally surrendered only in exchange for the highest price Man can pay, the wedding ring (although admittedly thousands of girls are swindled out of theirs every year). Even those impatient maidens who refuse to wait for marriage, do not rush pell-mell to rid themselves of their treasure with the first comer. On the contrary, they attach a certain importance to the How, and the Where, and the with Whom.

Having lost their virginity, the male with relief, the female with trepidation, are they at last on an equal footing? The answer is No.

Convention frowns on a woman's tenth transgression more severely than on her first. No matter how far removed from virginity she may be—married, widowed, divorced, or carefree—Society insists that the same high value continue to attach to her person. Only in exchange for a lifetime guarantee of security may she properly give herself.

The value of the male's body remains constant at zero. There is in fact a worldwide custom, so old that its origins are lost in antiquity, whereby a man induces a woman to give herself to him in exchange for gold or some other agreeable reward. So common is this procedure, so firmly rooted and accepted, that business establishments * have been founded, and fortunes made, by the practice of it on an organized basis. Man's body is held in such disrespect, it is taken for granted that he not only gives himself gratis, but that he must often bribe some disreputable woman to accept him; whereas the female is so highly prized that she is criticized for giving herself even when she receives generous payment in cash.

An extreme example of man's humility is his behavior in time of war, when by custom he ravishes any enemy woman who falls into his hands. In making her a present of himself, he feels he is insulting her and her whole nation. Is it possible to imagine a man and his nation feeling insulted if these positions were reversed? And is there a woman alive who would seek to humiliate an enemy soldier by forcing her favors on him?

Man's attitude toward Marriage further demonstrates his conviction that man is cheap, woman dear. Witness the enormous responsibilities he assumes, and the sacrifices he makes, in order to obtain exclusive rights to one woman.

It is true that the Double Standard creates an artificial set of values. So, too, does the Gold Standard—with the difference that gold actually is scarce. But the fact that these values are internationally respected makes them real enough. Ratio of utility to market price, the law of supply and demand, intrinsic worth, all are magnificently ignored, and no reevaluation is likely to take place in our time.

Once basic standards have been established, they must not be lightly overthrown, for they are the foundation on which are erected important economic and sociologic laws.

 These flourish in all civilizations, even those most dissimilar to ours. Only among savages is it unknown.

A sensible woman would no more favor abandoning the Double Standard than the United States would advocate going off the gold standard.

It is amusing to observe the contrariness of Man as he tries to induce us to break the very laws he himself invented and so stubbornly insists on maintaining. One can only suppose that he endorses these laws solely for the protection of his own women—*his* sister, *his* daughters, *his* wife—and the devil take all other men's sisters and daughters and wives. Or is it that with sheer masculine perversity he makes rules he has no intention of obeying, so that in the breaking of them his pleasure may be increased?

The man who tells you that chastity is an obsolete commodity has an ulterior reason. His aim is to reduce the importance of your gift in your own eyes, hoping thus to make you less hesitant to part with it—or having parted, less likely to expect anything in return. I say, heed him not.

And for heaven's sake

Fasten Your Chastity Belts!

SEVENTEEN

What to Do If You Didn't

tsk

tsk tsk

Now THEN, let us tsk no more tsks in vain regret or self-recrimination. Although you ignored, or found yourself unable to follow, the advice dispensed in the preceding chapter, although you are guilty of committing a tactical blunder of the highest order, the game is not yet lost. There is, alas, no known way to undo what you have done *—you can only try to make the best of it.

 Some, who have flexible consciences, seek to right matters by pretending to be what they no longer are. It is to be hoped they will protect more fastidiously their false virginity than they did their true.

171

Firstly and immediately

DECLARE YOURSELF IN LOVE

Swear that you love your seducer. Love is the only legitimate excuse for your misbehavior. Love has a way of purifying any sinful act. One who perjures, steals, or kills in the name of True Love is never as blameworthy as one who commits the same crimes for a less admirable reason. Love is the great whitewash.

Simultaneously,

EMPHASIZE THE VALUE OF YOUR GIFT

Do not act as if nothing has happened. Any hint that you consider your misdeed the Most Natural Thing in the World will be extremely disappointing to your seducer. No man appreciates having his triumph minimized or tossed off lightly.

Secondly,

REPEAT YOUR MISDEED

—with the same man * of course. This is not as easy as it sounds, for it is a fairly common masculine practice to abandon the victim after the victory, and many a girl finds herself in the pitiable plight of having lost not only her virtue but her man as well. To be taken once and then abandoned is a disgrace that can never be wiped off your memory book, and should be in itself enough to frighten a girl into behaving properly.

 It is to be hoped no girl will be so careless as to make the identical blunder with a different man.

If this misfortune does not befall you, be grateful and do not make the error of refusing to repeat the misdeed (except in the very particular instance which is described later on). Once the Privilege is granted him, a man is piqued if it is withdrawn, and he is likely to retaliate by dropping you. You must make every effort to encourage the wild shoot to take root and develop into a sturdy affair. With time on your side you may be able to win your seducer in marriage—the only way possible for a seduced girl to get even.

Bringing your seducer to the altar

Having established a steady relationship, almost any one of the 33 standard Methods can be called into play. There are also 4 Stratagems which are the special province of the seduced girl: Tragedietta, Caprice, Mea Culpa, and Gloriana.

1. *Tragedietta.* You are so remorseful, so ashamed of your transgression, you cannot face yourself in the mirror. You hint at suicide, you threaten to retire from the world, you tug at his heartstrings with tears of regret and mourning (which may, nay *should* be genuine) and declare that only marriage can wipe out your sin. You scream and wail and cry to heaven. You play your tragic role to the hilt, and if he is a man of humane instinct, and if he finds some pleasure in your embraces, there is a remote possibility that you will be able to attach a happy ending to your little tragedy.

2. *Caprice.* You are wistfully sad, yet strangely happy— much as if a beloved granduncle has died and left you a fortune. You regard your seducer with tender reproach and

rueful adoration. You shout invective at him one moment, and smother him with kisses the next. You vow, with every repetition of the sin, never to do it again, and he cannot be certain that each time is not the last. So bewildered is he, so unnerved with not knowing where he stands, that he may rush to the altar to find peace of mind.

3. *Mea Culpa.* If the debut was a failure, you insist it was your fault.* With delicate humbleness you blame it all on

 A girl should always take the blame for a failure except if the man is a Mr. A, B, C, or D, in which case, faced with certain abandonment, her only course is to lie ruthlessly. She must imply that it was he who was at fault. Gently forgiving, she tells her seducer that she understands. That she has heard that such things happen. That he can be sure she will not tell a soul. All this will drive a Mr. A crazy. Unable to walk away from such a challenge, he will return again and again to prove himself—and who knows where it will all end.

your qualms, your innocence, your asthma. Should the man you succumbed to be a Mr. O, or such, you will endear yourself by absolving him of all responsibility, and give yourself at least an outside chance of becoming Mrs. O, or such.

4. *Gloriana*. Your debut was a smashing success. You are that one couple out of 1,001 who are ideally mated. That rare and precious thing, a perfect union, is yours. He is all too aware that this is all too rare, and you know he will cut his throat rather than give you up. Here is "the very particular instance" in which a seduced girl may refuse to repeat her misdeed. You plead a tortured conscience, a fear of perdition, or whatever, and vow you will never again be alone with him until you are married. This stratagem accounts for some of those sudden marriages which occur after a few days of courtship.

Irrespective of which Method or Stratagem is used, there should be added (if not already present) a quantity of tempestuous emotion and spontaneous excitement. Make these lively ingredients an integral part of every encounter with your sweetheart, for a smooth-running, well-bred affair soon sinks into routine, and routine is death to Romance.

Unremitting vigilance is necessary to keep an affair interesting and untouched by staleness, and though the tone depends somewhat on the personality of the seducer, the prime factor, in the end, is the seduced girl's deportment.

Good deportment for naughty girls

A great deal has been written on this subject down through the ages. Skipping the classics, the first title that

175

comes to mind is the widely read *Good Bediquette,* which has much to offer. Martha Jane Hollaway's *Erotica for Advanced Girls* is another popular manual. Personally, I have found most helpful a little volume called *Good Manners for Every Occasion,* written some time ago by that redoubtable Englishwoman, Lady Dreadnought, as a guide for young gentlemen and ladies who are courting.

Lady Dreadnought, though very modern for her era, was far too proper to allow the word "bedroom" to drop from her quill. But one may extract nuggets of wisdom from her chapter on "Correct Deportment in the Ballroom" which is here quoted:

Rule 1: Be ladylike. This is not to say you must be prim. Many erringly believe that a lady cannot abandon herself to pleasure. Tut! The difference between a lady and a peasant is that a lady abandons herself after the manner of a lady, and a peasant abandons herself after the manner of a peasant. If you would please your partner, by all means abandon yourself to the excitement of the exercise, to the rhythm and the joy of it—but, pray never allow yourself to be vulgar.

If you scarce can breathe, gasp daintily for breath—do not groan. If your partner should murmur some humorous ditty in your ear, smile, or laugh softly—do not disturb the romantic atmosphere with hearty guffaws.

If you are guilty of a misstep, if you stumble or lose the beat, you need only blush delicately, eyes downcast—do not exclaim, or utter some crude banality like "Oops" or "Beg pardon."

Rule 2: Be modest. Prompted by a wish to titillate her partner's eye, a young lady sometimes oversteps the bounds of modesty. There is no call to present to view an undue amount of fair flesh. Lady Fashion smiles on a certain degree of nakedness, but Sir Sagacious tells us that subtle concealment is more alluring than frank revealment. La! Your true coquette understands this well, and tho' she display her prettiest parts with some daring whilst dancing, she draws a light veil or shawl about her so soon as the number is ended. The memory of a pink curve, now peek-a-booing thru fine lace, now discreetly covered, will, I daresay, be more distracting to your partner than unabashed, monotonous exposure. To say nothing of the danger of taking a chill.

Rule 3: Be feminine. If your partner did not have a preference for the fairer sex, he would take his entertainment with men. Behave, therefore, as much like a girl as you can. Do not try to lead or take the initiative. 'Tis the man's prerogative.

Do not correct his dancing unless he asks you to do so. Do not complain or yawn if he dances poorly.

Rule 4: Be romantic. Were a man interested in naught but the physical exercise, he would betake himself to a dancing academy where, for a fee, he could romp through the night with a professional partner. But the pastime is more pleasurable to a man when the girl he holds charges no fee, looks upon him adoringly, rests her little hand trustingly in his, and vows she would be happy forever, tripping the light fantastic with him.

Never allow the attention to wander, lest your dancing become mechanical and uninspired.

—Nor chatter and gossip. It spoils the mood.

—Nor let the gentleman see you are full of energy and ready

for another whirl, if he is noticeably exhausted.

—Nor let him suspect that you are tired, when he, apparently, is not. (Such frankness is permissible between married couples only.)

Rule 5: Be polite. Alas and alack, all too often partners are ill-suited to one another, and the moments spent vis-à-vis are a trial and a boredom, rather than a sweet experience. In such case a young lady ought spare her partner's feelings. Just as the courteous maiden will exclaim with delight over the bonbons brought by an admirer, whether they appeal to her palate or no—so should you give pleasure to your partner by feigning heavenly joy when none is felt. If, perchance, he is unaware that all is not going well, and, smiling blissfully to himself, imagines you are as satisfied as he, take your cue from him. Match him smile for smile, sigh for sigh, ooh for ah. Suffer his shortcomings—and your own —to pass unacknowledged, for without the burden of dispiriting truths both participants are more apt to improve. It is a shame and a pity to cut off a likely admirer because of a bad beginning, when with practice and patience you may eventually do well enough together.

Rule 6: Be amenable. The ideal partner is ready at all times to adapt herself to her escort's whims. If, in a moment of gaiety and madness he wishes to dance you off the dance floor, and twirl you out to the veranda, and down along the garden path, and onto the tulip bed, and beside the lily pond—yea, and even *in* the lily pond—do not demur. Be you as free and joyful as he, and he will be so enchanted he will want no other partner but you.

'Tis necessary, now and then, to break Rule 6 in order to observe Rule 1, and vice versa. There are some gentlemen who, tired of the amusements of their own class, relish an occasional fling at folk dancing. A well-mannered young lady must decide for herself whether to hearken to Rule 1 or Rule 6. Mayhap, in our disordered modern society, she will find that the man with whom she is frolicking is, in fact, a peasant. Should she excuse herself, pleading a weak ankle? Or should she suit her style to his? Each must find the answer in her own bonnet—remembering, of course, that today's dancing partner may turn out to be tomorrow's husband.

Oh, I could go on and on, quoting Lady Dreadnought. But that is the sort of thing that makes for a lazy writer. Suffice it to say that from a standpoint of good taste and good fun, Lady D.'s treatise on deportment in the ballroom may well be regarded as a model for standard deportment in *any* room.

To maintain a constant atmosphere of Romance and Beauty is a wearisome chore, to be sure, and imposes quite a strain on one. But, Sin is no cinch, and when a girl leaves the easy path of Virtue, she must expect to encounter hardships.

CAUTION. While exerting every effort to charm and beguile, you must at the same time be careful not to make Sir Seducer too comfortable. A man who lacks for nothing has no incentive to marry. On the contrary, he resists the idea of even a slight change in the status quo. For this reason it is a fatal mistake to spend the night in his apartment, or to let him spend the night in yours.

So long as a man must rouse himself from a cozy nap, and put on all his clothes, and take his guest all the way home, and then travel all the way back to his empty apartment,

and take off all his clothes, and get back into bed again—he will not be completely content with the arrangement (especially in nasty weather), and may in desperation seize upon marriage as a time- and energy-saver.

Moreover, while a woman is happiest lying free and un-crowded in her bed at night, a man sleeps most soundly when he is clutching his bedmate in an iron grip. Grant the bachelor this last blessed relief from his aloneness, and you give up your most powerful argument for matrimony.

There are two possible endings to a Seduction.

     a. It results in marriage.
     b. It does not.

To the girl who wins the happy ending, I extend my congratulations.

To those far more numerous girls whose misdeeds end in disappointment, I can only say, "I told you so."

EIGHTEEN

Pitfalls and How to Avoid Them

Do NOT allow yourself to become so intent on setting Traps and brewing Potions, that you fail to see the Pitfalls that lie all about you. Forewarned is forearmed. I therefore list here the twelve errors that are most commonly made, with instructions on how to avoid them.*

1. Sounding the tocsin

A. *Do Not Create Rumors of Marriage.* Do not give out interim reports to friends or family, no matter how anxiously

 When these instructions conflict with the Method you are using, they are to be ignored. Method Always Comes First.

they question you. To say that you "think he is serious" or it "looks as if he might be getting ready to propose" gives rise to premature cheering which may reach his ears and alert him to his danger.

B. *Train Your Family to Be Tactful.* Warn parents, sisters, brothers, and household help that they are not to regard him with knowing looks or self-conscious smiles, nor introduce him as "Joan's young man" or "the young man Joan is ... uh ... going to ... uh ..." nor overwhelm him with friendly attentions. A little discreet antagonism is less likely to scare him off than an over-eager welcome.

C. *Avoid the Symbols of Marriage.* Never—NEVER—lead a man toward a display of wedding cakes, bridal veils, or

baby clothes. Do not even stop to look into a jeweler's window, for the sight of but one wedding ring nestling among a hundred harmless baubles can have so electrifying an effect on the sensitive nerves of a male that he may vanish from your side and never be seen again.

2. Being too honest

With success in sight one sometimes grows careless. A girl who has hewn to the line of her Method and unfailingly concealed all her faults throughout an arduous campaign, may one day let down her guard and in a moment of snug intimacy give away information that can hurt her cause.

Until you feel the sweet weight of his wedding ring on your finger, remain vigilant. Do not reveal that you are lazy, spendthrift, finicky, self-indulgent, argumentative, stubborn, quick-tempered, and fickle. Do not give any hint that you intend to stop working at the sound of the wedding bell, that you cannot abide his family, that you have a number of old debts you have been saving for your husband. Do not confide that you lied—about your age, or your bank account, or your past.

Do not, in short, provide him with a reason to back out of his contract before he has signed it!

3. Falling in love

La Rochefoucald wrote, "The pleasure of love is in loving." Nonsense! I do not like to challenge one I hold in high esteem, particularly when he is no longer here to defend himself, but I must speak out. Girls, do not believe M. La R. There is no joy in loving if the loved one does not return your love.

However, it is my purpose to deal here not with the emotional delights but the practical aspects of the Male/Female connection. And nothing could be more impractical than loving someone who a) loves you not, or b) loves you not enough. It puts the whip in his hand and leaves you powerless. What can you refuse him? What need has he to surrender his freedom?

Keep your affections under control. Save your love for your husband, the only man who is really entitled to it.

If you cannot refrain from loving an undeserving stranger, have the good sense to hide your weakness and try to conduct your courtship in a businesslike manner.

4. Being possessive

A good way to drive a man away is by taking possession of his possessions. Even though he offers the use of his car or motorcycle, a girl who has her wits about her will not accept. She will not borrow his golf clubs, his shirts, his camera. She will not transfer his books and records from his house to hers. She will not clutter his closets and bureaus with things she has moved from her house to his.

The male does not like to share his possessions. He cherishes his privacy and his belongings. Knowing this, does it not seem foolish to give him fair warning of what he may expect from a wife? How much better to let him discover after it is too late, that in marriage there is no such thing as private ownership, that all he has—even his dearest souvenirs—must be shared, that nothing will ever again be exclusively his.

5. Being too clever

The most ignorant female is often cleverer than the most learned male. Revealing this cleverness has cost many a girl her final victory.

If you can easily see through a man's lies, subterfuges, and deceits, close your eyes.

If you can anticipate what he will do or say, or guess the endings to all his jokes, hold your tongue.

If you can detect errors in his arithmetic or etiquette, or flaws in his memory, do not catch him up on it.

No man wants a wife he cannot fool, or one who anticipates him, or knows more than he does about anything.

"That maid who is too clever, will remain a maid forever."
—M. K. STRATFORD

6. *Going steady too long*

Going steady gives a girl the opportunity to work her Method, and at the same time affords her the convenience of an escort for every occasion. Despite these advantages one must not allow the arrangement to continue indefinitely. The man takes no risks, assumes no obligations, and when he becomes bored with his steady girl, or interested in another, he is free to walk away.

If you cannot, within a reasonable period, extract an engagement ring from one who selfishly engages your time and affections, give him up. The title "Steady Girl" is without honor and without status in serious circles.

7. *Extended engagements*

During the time of the engagement it sometimes happens that a man recovers from the sudden weakness, the fever that caused him to surrender himself. One month, two months, possibly three, pass by in a euphoric dream—and

then comes a cooling-off period. Beware! Do not let this period go on too long. The betrothed man's heart is too often overflowing with regrets. He is wretched because he allowed himself to be caught, and he sees as an imminent reality the hitherto vaguely dreaded burdens of marriage. He recognizes that his Promised Bride is an albatross whose weight he must carry about all his life, and he begins to resent her as much as if she were already his wife.

Since he is subject to many of the restrictions of marriage, he has the rebellious instincts normally expected only in a husband. He looks upon other girls with longing; because they are forbidden they appear to be much more desirable than the one to whom he is bound. In this frame of mind a man may allow himself to be "rescued" from the very jaws of matrimony by some strange female who seems to him, in his fuddled condition, preferable to his Enemy, the Betrothed. He is too distraught to comprehend that he is merely changing his owner, not cheating his destiny.

More frequently, however, the man-too-long-engaged completely loses his appetite for entanglements of any kind. The longer the engagement drags on, the harder it is for him to remember what inflamed him, what made him agree to marriage in the first place.

Dear Reader, do not let him reach this shiveringly low temperature. Strike while the iron is hot! It may seem important that you wait until he gets his degree, builds up his savings account, finds a better job, or comes into his inheritance. But not one of these things is worth the risk.

☞ Marry first, make improvements later

8. Socializing with his friends and relatives

Last one in is a rotten egg. That is how a man's friends and relatives look upon his girl. She is the stranger, the intruder, and with the cliquishness common to all mankind, they band together to prevent her from entering their coterie.

His unmarried friends, fearful of losing their playmate once he enters the dark abyss of marriage, employ insidious propaganda against the interloper. His married friends regard her as a thief who would rob them of the precious bachelor they have earmarked for some needy sister or cousin of their own. His parents and relatives are particularly resentful of this girl who thinks she is good enough to bear their name. Though their relative be the fool on the family tree, still he is one of their own and hardly anyone seems fit to share a branch with him.

A girl who has a man's family and friends pulling against her, faces an almost unbeatable team. All her Lures and Traps and Spells are examined and exposed by his protectors, who can of course see them more objectively than the victim. Every moment he is away from her, others are undoing and destroying her careful work. No man can withstand so much opposition unless he is fortified by an imperishable love for the girl, or by an intense desire to spite his dear ones.

A friendless orphan is ideal husband material, but these are rare and one must work with what is available. Abstain, therefore, from socializing with and, if possible, from so much as meeting with a man's friends and relatives, for they are almost certain to kill your chances.

9. *Letting him socialize with yours*

It would seem that a girl could count on her own friends and relatives to assist her in capturing the man she wants. Yet, sometimes with the best intentions—and sometimes, alas, with the worst—they are guilty of driving him away.

The danger of too much warmth is described in Pitfall 1. Equally dangerous is too much coolness. Fathers are the worst offenders in this department. Eager though a father may be to have a daughter taken off his hands, he cannot but eye the prospective taker with dislike. He remembers the worries and the costs of bringing his darling child from whimpering infanthood to simpering young ladyhood, and regrets having gone to such pains just to provide some stranger with a wife. He broods over the thought of his baby girl cooking and cleaning for this nobody, picking up after him, doing all kinds of things to please him, treating him,

in fact, better than she ever treated her good old dad. Is it any wonder then that the jealous parent insults and discourages perfectly acceptable young men?

Father is not the only troublemaker. Mother too can ruin a budding match. How many women look at their precious offspring and vow, "She's going to get something better than I got!" and they drive away their daughters' suitors. But there is not always something better to be had, and by the time Mother is ready to compromise, the years may have depreciated daughter's value to a point where she will be happy to settle for something far worse than what Mother got.

As to sisters—a sister cannot always be trusted, for who knows what secret rivalries and jealousies may cause her to sabotage a promising match.

Actually you must be on guard against all females, most

especially those who find a thousand things to criticize in your beau, and speak of him so disparagingly that any self-respecting girl would be ashamed to marry him. (Often such a critic will belittle a man with the hope of catching him for herself after she has tricked you into discarding him.)

Keep all contact between your beaux and your intimates down to a minimum. Brief greetings, fleeting peeks, are sufficient. Socializing can only lead to disaster. Even if you are certain that your family will love and welcome any man who looks as if he might marry you, you do not know if he will return their affection. Unless your relatives are really delightful,* exposure is unwise. Nothing depresses a man so much as a foretaste of a dreary future with a pack of drab or uncouth in-laws.

Take heed. If your relatives are repulsive, it is all right to love them, but for goodness sake keep them hidden until the wedding day.

10. Inviting competition

Common sense will warn every girl to avoid comparisons that do not show her in a favorable light. If your sister is a beauty, your cousin an heiress, your friend a sparkling personality, your neighbor a seductress, keep them away from your admirers. Surround yourself only with females whose attractions can be dimmed by your own. Affections are too easily transferred, loyalties too quickly forgotten. In the struggle to win a man, not even one's own widowed mother can be counted on.

 In which case you will put them to good use as described in Spellbinder #5.

11. *Too much propinquity*

The advantages of Propinquity are self-evident. However, I needs must cry Caution. There is such a thing as too much Propinquity.

Some girls seem nice only if taken in small doses. Otherwise they turn out to be dull or disagreeable. If you know that you do not wear well, avoid spending prolonged evenings alone with a man you are trying to catch. Arrange always to be at a place of public entertainment with him, or in the midst of a crowd of people. Stay close enough so that he cannot be lost or stolen but not so close that he will become bored. If you manage to distract him with other people and other things he will be less apt to tire of you.

Even if you are adorable at all times, too much Propinquity will rob you of the qualities of newness and mystery which a man finds so appealing. If he gets too much of you he will inevitably come to regard you as predictable, familiar, and unexciting. This is all very well after you become his wife. It is standard. But if he feels that way *before*, there is unlikely to be an *after*.

12. *Too much apartness*

There is an old saying—
Absence Makes the Heart Grow Fonder
and there is another saying—
Absence Is the Enemy of Love.

Which is true? Both. This must be so, for the wisdom of the ages is contained in adages and old wives' tales. Trust them before you trust your doctors, scientists, psychologists, philosophers, savants, and those authorities who write magazine articles.

But, you may ask, if absence makes the heart grow

fonder, how can it also be the enemy of love? The following story will illustrate:

A girl named Mildred (she is the sister of that girl who took my cousin Randolph by means of The Great Deception) knew a taxidermist named Harald. Fairly early in their acquaintance Harald went to the North Pole to study polar bears—their habits, their postures, their interiors— and Mildred, using the Woodpecker Formula, wrote him many long, friendly letters. To her joy, Harald responded with enthusiasm and showed far more warmth in the Arctic than he had in Omaha, Nebraska. Through the six-months-long night his letters grew more frequent and more ardent, and it was certainly clear that with Absence, his Heart had Grown Fonder.

Then the darkness ended. Day came and Harald saw igloos in the distance. Hungry for human companionship he went visiting. In the very first igloo he entered he met an Eskimo girl, who invited him to have some walrus stew, and here is where Absence Makes the Heart Grow Fonder stopped working and Absence is the Enemy of Love took over. Had Mildred been on the scene she might very well have held her own against Ekbu. But her Absence worked against her and Propinquity worked in favor of her Eskimo rival, who is a prime example of a girl being at the right place at the right time. In all probability Harald would have married Ekbu if he had not been eaten by an indignant bear.

However, that is not the point of the story. The point is that the philosophy behind each proverb, though contradictory and obscure, is true. It requires a little insight to interpret wisdom that has been compressed to fit into a nutshell. But clever sayings must be succinct. People do not like to quote a proverb like: Absence is the enemy of love when there are other girls available in the place where he is and you are not, for the heart cannot tolerate a vacuum and if it is not filled with one thing then it must be filled with another. Still, I suggest that you paste it in your memory book and refer to it often if ever you try to capture a man from a distance.

There are other pitfalls, but the twelve analyzed here cause the greatest amount of trouble. Eliminate this devilish dozen from your path and you will have removed some of the worst hazards that a girl faces on the road to matrimony.

NINETEEN

Kindness in Victory

EVERY GIRL is entitled to a husband and I pray that each of you will get the kind you dream of getting. But if you do not, it will not surprise me. Being a girl simply entitles you to a husband—not a *good* husband or a *darling* husband or a *rich* husband or a *faithful* husband, but just A HUSBAND.

Hardly anyone ever gets what she deserves, or thinks she deserves. For there simply are not enough wealthy healthy charming intelligent generous attractive men in existence. Look at the husbands of your friends, relatives, and neighbors. What did *they* get? A girl who sincerely wants to be married accepts the fact that in taking a husband one must compromise. It is, after all, better to be married to someone a little less than your ideal than not to be married at all.

Long long ago, when Babylon was a great metropolis, an ancient savant wrote in the Mishnah that the woman who marries herself to an ant is better off than the one who remains a spinster. Most women are born with this knowledge on the tip of their minds. Others, who through some congenital fault are born without it, learn it through experience, and sometimes too late.

It is, I grant you, most discouraging to look about at the men who fill the world. How self-centered they seem, and bad-mannered and arrogant and unromantic and conceited and stubborn and belligerent, and spoiled and greedy and generally disappointing.

But one fateful day, from the midst of the crowd, one of these unworthy creatures will turn around and look at you with interest. Lo! he is magically changed at once. He is clever and charming and noble and kind (though to your father, and even perhaps to his own, he seems an absolute noodle) and you want him for your very own.

If he tries to run away, if he hides and struggles and defies you, and in the end must be carried kicking and screaming to the altar, blame him not. The men of America have ever loved liberty.

Remember as you walk up the aisle to the triumphant strains of the Wedding March, that the quaking bridegroom who waits you at the other end is no longer your adversary, strong, elusive, defiant, but your captive, your slave—and vow that you will be good to him:

That you will often soften your commands with sweet words like "dear" or "honey"—that you will now and then reward his industry and his faithfulness with a gentle pat or a kiss—that you will provide him with enough pocket money to buy a pack of cigaretters or a newspaper whenever he so desires—that you will close the windows when you have to scold him, and never chastise him in front of his friends—that sometimes you will smile at him for no reason at all—that you will let him have a few hours each week to do with as he wishes—that you will in all matters let him have his say, although final decisions rest with you—that you will comfort, pet, praise, and coddle him at least five minutes every day, and make him feel that he is wanted and needed and loved.

FOR

if you do not treat him well, he may run away from home, and you will lose what you fought so hard to win.

I have no wish to conclude this book on a sad note, and will not therefore quote the statistics on how many mistreated husbands desert their wives each year. But the number is frightening. Always bear this in mind.

Remember, too, that a slave crushed and demeaned is no credit to his mistress. But one who walks with pride and dignity, who reflects the good treatment and generous care accorded him by a magnanimous conqueror, and who never ceases to sing his lady's praises—that slave will bring glory to his household.

For these reasons I beg all brides to rule with a soft tongue, to forget (whenever possible) old animosities and resentments, and to invest the rank of Husband with a degree of honor and respectability.

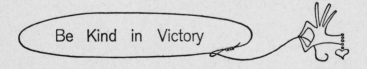

Be Kind in Victory

ABOUT THE AUTHOR

Nina Farewell, in answer to our request for a photograph, replied, "I have rummaged about for a flattering old portrait, and what I have decided to send you are these quotes from the word picture I supplied for The Unfair Sex:

"'... must confess I am terribly attractive ... complexion flawless from head to toe ... teeth, to borrow a simile, like pearls ... eyes defy description ... nose adorable ... curves intelligently distributed ... I am elegant enough to intrigue the most vulgar of men, vulgar enough to enchant the most cultured, and never have I embarrassed any man by knowing as much as he did about anything.'

"This was written in 1953 and naturally I have aged two or three years since then, but on the whole the description is as accurate now as it ever was."

Going further, Nina Farewell answers some intimate questions for us.

On Pets: No animal is as lovable and companionable as a man. For the perfect pet give me a husband any time.

On Hobbies: I simply adore ancient man, and the study of him is my favorite hobby. Many people, including myself, are astonished by my knowledge of ancient history. I am not good on names and dates, but rarely do I forget a face.

On Working Habits: I keep to a rigid schedule—two hours each day, rain or snow. (In clear, sunny weather I do not touch my pen.) My writing method is simple. I just jot down one thought after another, then I gather up all the papers and take them over to my old grammar-school teacher, and she puts in the spelling and punctuation.